What Your Colleagues Are Saying . . .

"It's a comfort knowing that, at last, there's a book about close reading that honors and respects the needs of teachers in the intermediate grades. You will read, dog-ear pages, study the book with team members, and revisit and reread parts on your own. It is a must-have book for your professional library and for professional learning communities!"

—LAURA ROBB, Author of *Unlocking Complex Texts*

"Nancy Boyles does a superb job of explaining close reading and when teachers should have students engage with it. Through the wealth of practical teaching ideas she offers herein, she reminds us that reading is purpose-driven. . . . The result is that teachers and students alike understand when to read close and, as important, not so close!"

—MICHAEL F. OPITZ, Coauthor of *Good-Bye Round Robin,* Updated Edition

"This is the book you have been waiting for! With keen insight and explicit attention to detail, Nancy Boyles provides the resources you need, just when you need them. *Closer Reading* is a must-have for all literacy leaders, administrators, and teachers who want to see their students gain a deeper understanding of reading comprehension."

—CATHY MASTRIANNA, President of Connecticut Reading Association

"Nancy Boyles' *Closer Reading, Grades 3–6* is my new go-to book for sorting through the myths, mystique, uncertainties, and questions surrounding the close reading of complex text and, more important, the positioning of readers, writers, learners, and teachers as they navigate close reading within and beyond a standards-based curriculum."

—JANE WELLMAN-LITTLE, President of New England Reading Association

"Nancy's ability to 'sit on your shoulder' as she guides you to understand the real meaning of close reading, choose appropriate text for an authentic purpose, and assess its effectiveness—all while building on our prior knowledge and affirming our passion and commitment to be better teachers—is like no other . . . This outstanding resource is a must-have professional text."

—BARBARA E. MECHLER, Assistant Superintendent of Schools, New Fairfield, CT

"Dr. Nancy Boyles combines her vast knowledge of literacy, the Common Core State Standards, and best practices for students as she guides our understanding of close reading: what it is, what it isn't, and how to embed it into daily instruction. . . . This book is a treasure of knowledge and practical teaching practices that won't collect dust on any shelf in your classroom."

—JEN TAPIA, Director of Professional Development for Aurora Public Schools, IL

CLOSER
Reading
GRADES 3–6

In loving memory of my wonderful grandmother, Vernie Elizabeth Baldwin

August 27, 1903–March 4, 2002

She truly was that kind of lady

CLOSER Reading

GRADES 3–6

Better Prep, **Smarter** Lessons, **Deeper** Comprehension

NANCY **BOYLES**

FOREWORD BY
LAURA **ROBB**

CORWIN
A SAGE Company

FOR INFORMATION:

Corwin
A SAGE Company
2455 Teller Road
Thousand Oaks, California 91320
(800) 233-9936
www.corwin.com

SAGE Publications Ltd.
1 Oliver's Yard
55 City Road
London EC1Y 1SP
United Kingdom

SAGE Publications India Pvt. Ltd.
B 1/I 1 Mohan Cooperative Industrial Area
Mathura Road, New Delhi 110 044
India

SAGE Publications Asia-Pacific Pte. Ltd.
3 Church Street
#10-04 Samsung Hub
Singapore 049483

Publisher: Lisa Luedeke
Development Editor: Wendy Murray
Editorial Development Manager: Julie Nemer
Editorial Assistant: Francesca Dutra Africano
Production Editor: Melanie Birdsall
Copy Editor: Linda Gray
Typesetter: C&M Digitals (P) Ltd.
Proofreader: Caryne Brown
Indexer: Karen Wiley
Cover and Interior Designer: Janet Kiesel

Photographs by Matt Hanley, East Aurora School District 131.

Clipart used with permission of www.clipart.com.

Printed in the United States of America

Library of Congress Cataloging-in-Publication Data

Boyles, Nancy N.

Closer reading, grades 3-6 : better prep, smarter lessons, deeper comprehension / Nancy Boyles.

pages cm
Includes bibliographical references and index.

ISBN 978-1-4833-0445-8 (pbk.)

1. Language arts—Standards—United States. 2. English language—Study and teaching—Standards—United States. I. Title.

LB1576.B545 2014
372.6—dc23   2013040356

This book is printed on acid-free paper.

Certified Chain of Custody
Promoting Sustainable Forestry
www.sfiprogram.org
SFI-01268
SFI label applies to text stock

14 15 16 17 18 10 9 8 7 6 5 4 3 2 1

Contents

CHAPTER 7. MOVING STUDENTS TOWARD INDEPENDENCE IN CLOSE READING   117

CHAPTER 8. DIGGING DEEPER IN CLOSE READING THROUGH REREADING, SMALL-GROUP INSTRUCTION, AND INDEPENDENT READING   129

CHAPTER 9. CLOSE READING FOR THE COMMON CORE—AND MORE   155

APPENDICES

Visit the companion website at
www.corwin.com/closerreading
for downloadable resources.

Foreword

Every teacher in Grades 3 to 6 needs a copy of Nancy Boyles's book. *Closer Reading, Grades 3–6* will become teachers' road map for helping their intermediate grade students develop the art of close reading with success and joy, and, at the same time, move students deeper and deeper into powerful texts. Throughout this book, Nancy Boyles uses her strong and passionate teacher's voice to include you in her wise advice and practical examples. Open your door and let Nancy enter your classroom. Why? Because she'll be by your side talking to you, explaining, coaching, cheering you on as you refine and adjust your teaching practices to meet Common Core close reading guidelines—and all in an atmosphere of common sense and sensitivity to teachers' needs. Yes, common sense because Nancy has grounded her book in solid research, in her past and current teaching experiences, and in her knowledge of what deep, analytical comprehension, or close reading, means for teachers who have classes of students at diverse reading levels.

In this outstanding and readable book, Nancy takes teachers on a learning journey. She starts by building a bridge of understanding that connects what teachers know and have done as reading instructors to the Common Core's concept of close reading. Moreover, Nancy has carefully thought about each chapter's topic, positioning information so that it enhances teachers' ability to understand close reading in order to adjust and, at times, change their practice.

After a clear explanation of close reading, Nancy presents the Common Core's take on text complexity, and then she adds top-notch tips that enable teachers to choose complex texts for their students. She shows teachers how to design a close reading lesson, makes the planning clear and accessible, and includes a template to guide you through the process.

The middle chapters show teachers how to design a close reading lesson that supports readers using the tried-and-true three-part model: before, during, and after reading. Like the master teacher she is, Nancy provides teachers with ways to move students to independence with close reading so they can apply what they've learned to texts they read on their own. Finally, she takes you deeper into close reading by showing how rereading, small-group instruction, and independent reading work in concert to enhance students' close reading stamina. These chapters focus on teaching students how to cite textual evidence, make logical inferences, notice text structure, and pinpoint themes; they also demonstrate the benefits and importance of structuring lessons so that students complete multiple readings of texts. You'll find a detailed chart that provides focus points for planning small-group lessons and for independent reading. This chart helps readers recognize how to apply the strategy and where in the text the strategy will most likely be applied. And always on center stage is the student and what each child requires to become a successful close reader of complex texts.

And there's so much more that Nancy's book offers, all geared to supporting teachers:

- An extensive lesson plan for shared reading with a complex text that Nancy provides.
- A clear and friendly explanation that deepens teachers' understandings of the Common Core anchor standards for informational and literary texts.
- A chart that features the steps of the gradual release of teacher support to students.
- Annotated lists of Nancy's favorite complex texts that include picture and chapter books. She also includes websites for short texts!
- Guidelines that show students how to read like a scientist and historian and evaluate primary sources.
- Tips for reading a photograph, viewing a video, and looking at and learning from words and illustrations all support close reading.
- A detailed chart of open-ended close reading questions for literary and informational texts for each standard. This is a resource that teachers and students will use again and again.

Charts, templates, and graphics in the book can be found at **www.corwin.com/ closerreading** for you to download, print, or use on a whiteboard.

It's a comfort knowing that, at last, there's a book about close reading that honors and respects the needs of teachers in the intermediate grades. You will read, dog-ear pages, study the book with team members, and revisit and reread parts on your own. This book will become a treasured friend and guide, as you will value every tip, model lesson, and complex book recommendation. *Closer Reading, Grades 3–6* is a must-have book for your professional library and for professional learning communities!

—*Laura Robb*

Acknowledgments

I am grateful for the support of so many individuals for helping to make this book a reality:

Matt Hanley, Assistant Director of Community Relations, East Aurora, Illinois—for the dozens of fine photos he took, capturing the hard work of students and teachers in District 131 as they were engaged in close reading.

Jennifer Tapia, Coordinator of Professional Development for East Aurora—for setting up the photo sessions, gathering the hundreds of permission forms, and always setting up such productive professional development sessions for the staff in her district.

My students in the Graduate Reading Program at Southern Connecticut State University—for exploring with me, semester after semester, the intricacies of close reading.

The Corwin Literacy team—for your good work in countless ways, and for making this such a positive experience for me. I am especially grateful to:

Francesca Dutra Africano, Editorial Assistant—for your supreme efficiency.

Julie Nemer, Editorial Development Manager—for your design magic (a standout feature of Corwin books!).

Melanie Birdsall, Senior Project Editor—for coordinating all aspects of the publications phase and somehow making it look so easy.

Maura Sullivan, Marketing Strategist—for the great title!

Linda Gray—for your keen eye as a copy editor. I certainly appreciate that attention to detail.

Lisa Luedeke, Corwin Literacy Publisher and editor extraordinaire of this book—for your insights as both an editor and an educator. I have learned so much from sharing this journey with you and will be forever grateful for your thoughtful guidance.

Wendy Murray—for your eleventh-hour support and expertise. I am so grateful!

And above all, my husband, Ron Boyles: What would I do without your constant (and cheerful!) goodwill—not to mention your willingness to cook dinner, vacuum, and renovate a whole house every few years.

Introduction

Getting Closer

The goal of this book is simple: to build an understanding of close reading and how to teach close reading well. It's a worthy goal, and not just because the Common Core tells us that close reading is good for our students. It's worthy because close reading truly does help students probe a text more thoroughly for deep comprehension—with or without new standards. Close reading is a process worth the time and energy it takes to understand it because when we take it back to our classroom and apply it, we will see right away that it works. This book goes well beyond a description of *strategies* to *apply* to close reading. Rather, it shows you how to *teach* the art of close reading—with each chapter designed to take you one step closer to that goal.

Who Will Benefit From This Book?

This book is for anyone who wants to help students develop deeper reading comprehension through close reading. It is aimed most directly at elementary classroom teachers of Grades 3 through 6, with exemplars and supporting materials aligned to practices at the intermediate level. But teachers from the early primary grades to those who teach seventh and eighth graders will find the instructional practices useful in moving close reading forward in their grades too. Likewise, teachers of specialized populations and English learners will find guidance here. The same is true for teachers of high-performing students. Perhaps the emphasis on critical thinking will offer these students the additional rigor that will stretch the limits of even their thinking.

Reading specialists, consultants, and coaches have an especially important role to play in the implementation of close reading. First, it will be these school literacy leaders who provide direct services to students who struggle to meet the challenges of the Common Core through regular (Tier 1) classroom instruction. A thorough understanding of the close reading practices described in this book will build the solid foundation they need as they scaffold their Tier 2 and Tier 3 close reading interventions. Furthermore, literacy coaches are charged with supporting not only students but staff. With a clearer view of what to look for in standards-based close reading instruction, it will be easier for coaches to identify teachers' needs and to help address those needs.

Finally, this book is intended to guide building administrators who oversee their school's implementation of curriculum. Often, principals and assistant principals do not come to their roles via a route that includes current coursework in reading. It is difficult to guide and support what we do not understand. This book seeks to provide "helpful help" to busy administrators so they can hit the ground running with instructional leadership for close reading.

Whether you are a classroom teacher, a teacher who supports special populations of students, a school literacy leader, or a building administrator, this book will be a useful resource for reading thoughtfully and reflectively on your own or with other colleagues in your professional learning community. Each chapter ends with questions to aid you in such reflection.

Finding Our Starting Point

To reach our close reading destination, we need to set our personal navigation system from our current location: My starting point is now decades ago—as an elementary teacher of many grades. Even then, comprehension was the part I loved best about teaching reading. I remained in the classroom for many years despite the advanced degrees I eventually earned; I couldn't imagine a more meaningful place to be in education than right alongside children. When I moved to university teaching, comprehension was still my favorite part of the syllabus. Along the way, I have written several books, every one of them focused in some way on—you guessed it—comprehension. Additionally, I have the privilege of traveling about my state (Connecticut) and throughout the country, sharing my thoughts about comprehension at conferences, at institutes, and in district-sponsored professional development. Recently, of course, much of this conversation has turned to the Common Core and, in particular, close reading.

I am proud to say that my most cherished starting point remains the same as that of many of the educators who will hold this book: the classroom! I spend several days each week providing direct services to schools: doing model lessons, coaching teachers and literacy leaders, and meeting with school personnel to reflect on what works—and what doesn't—in powerful literacy instruction. Everything you read in this book I have tried personally in classrooms ranging from primary to middle school, within urban, suburban, and rural districts. These school visits keep me both honest and humble. I am gratified when kids and teachers thrive on a technique I have developed. Those strategies often find their way into a book. And then there are those "well, *that* didn't work" moments, where something that *sounds* really good on paper just doesn't make it in the classroom. You won't find any of those too-good-to-be-true great ideas here.

You have the Nancy Boyles pledge that the pages that follow don't just "sound good." The guiding principles, lesson, templates, charts, and other supports really do position you and your students to thrive as apprentices of close reading. I believe that the close reading practices described in this book are *best* practices. That does not mean, however, that my way is the *only way.* You may hear about other approaches to close reading, and you will need to decide for yourself whether they meet the criteria for accomplishing the same depth and breadth of understanding described in the chapters that follow.

Whoever you are or wherever you teach, I am confident you are bringing more to this close reading agenda than you anticipate. I've noticed as I've visited classrooms that teaching close reading brings out the best in teachers. It feels natural. It's the way many of us *like* to teach. And when *we* are happy in our work, our students are happy in their learning. I'm smiling already thinking about the joy of the journey ahead.

Let our journey toward closer reading begin.

Closer Reading

Closer Than What?

This book, *Closer Reading, Grades 3–6,* begs the question, closer than *what*? The short answer is, closer than past practice. My goal in writing this resource is to show teachers the benefits and how-to of close reading, but to do this in a manner that helps teachers, I also give my take on which past practices to keep, which to amplify, and which to recognize didn't work well and why. With or without the Common Core State Standards, close reading is a terrific long-lost cousin we are bringing back into our teaching lives. But to make room for it, we have to clearly define the instructional shifts we need to make.

Here is crux of what we need to reexamine about past reading practices: Despite that in recent years teachers and students have been meticulous about pursuing textual evidence to support their claims—answering such questions as, *In what ways did the main character show courage? What is the meaning of photosynthesis based on other words in the sentence? What is the main idea of paragraph two?*—it hasn't been enough to produce sufficient numbers of college-ready young adults. That is, while this comprehension of texts has been good enough to satisfy high school graduation requirements for lots of students, it hasn't impressed placement counselors at community colleges who tell us that nearly 70% of incoming freshmen require multiple semesters of remedial coursework before embarking on credit-bearing college courses. The percentage of unprepared students entering more selective colleges and universities is less grim, though some still require catch-up courses, which is a poor use of students' financial resources and an unflattering commentary on the academic preparation that brought them this far (*Beyond the Rhetoric*, n.d.).

I sigh when I hear these disappointing reports of older students' lackluster academic performance. When I am honest with myself, though, I know I can't entirely assert that students' reading performance began to falter only after they left my domain of elementary school, where the cups overflowed with the five pillars, a renaissance in children's literature, and strategy instruction. I have to accept some blame. We all do.

All of us in elementary education need to reflect on what may have gone awry, even with all our good intentions and hard work. Sure, we can't cure a recession, poverty, pared-down education budgets, politics, and all the rest. But we have to acknowledge that many of these poorly prepared college students also performed marginally in our eighth-grade language arts class, our fifth-grade classroom, and probably in the primary grades as well.

What went wrong? We teachers followed our district's literacy curriculum, scrutinized our data, implemented a thoughtful response to intervention plan, adhered—like glue—to the recommendations of the National Reading Panel (incorporating those famous five pillars: phonemic awareness, phonics, fluency, vocabulary, and comprehension), attended professional development sessions regularly, and probably juggled a hundred other mandates and edicts. We have worked incredibly hard on behalf of our students because we care about their success and believe passionately that we can make a difference.

Now the nation's governors and education commissioners through their representative organizations, the National Governors Association (NGA) and the Council of Chief State School Officers (CCSSO) have asked us to try one more thing in order to make a difference: the Common Core State Standards (CCSS). Signed into law by most states in 2010, these new standards have brought with them not only a progression of rigorous English Language Arts and Math standards for Grades K–12, but in their wake, a chorus of voices, each heralding advice about how best to teach to achieve these standards (though the Common Core doesn't actually prescribe any particular instructional methodology).

Amid the Common Core clamor, one practice that is championed by an array of educators and researchers is close reading. It's got a heft of research behind it, and it isn't new but harkens back to prior decades. Notice in the following quote that it is not *just* the close reading or *just* the complex text, but the combination of both that leads to college (and career) readiness.

> A significant body of research links the close reading of complex text— whether the student is a struggling reader or advanced—to significant gains in reading proficiency and finds close reading to be a key component of college and career readiness. (Partnership for Assessment of Readiness for College and Careers [PARCC], 2012, p. 7)

It would be naïve to think that any single instructional shift could lead to perfect preparation of all our high school graduates, but close reading, I sincerely believe, holds promise—if we get it right. Getting it right will require four central actions:

1. Understanding what close reading *is*
2. Tweaking past practices for better alignment to close reading
3. Envisioning an instructional model that includes close reading
4. Designing and implementing literacy lessons that embody the very best principles and practices of close reading

Understanding Close Reading

As I said, close reading is not a new term. This notion of close reading has been around for a long time, but it has generally been used to define a method of text analysis more common in high school and college than in elementary grades or middle school. Aligned with the "New Criticism," it was prevalent in the middle decades of the twentieth century, promoting the notion that "meaning existed on the page" and that reading well revealed "subtlety, unity, and integrity" (Abrams, 1999, pp. 180–182). For fellow French majors out there, the term *en français* is "explication de texte." Long ago when I was a French major, we applied it to Molière, Voltaire, Rousseau, and their contemporaries. Now we will get fourth graders to apply this to Cynthia Rylant, Seymour Simon, and Patricia MacLachlan.

We could define close reading in a simple, straightforward way as reading to uncover layers of meaning resulting in deep comprehension. That quite succinctly addresses the *intent* of close reading, but it misses the fine points describing just *how* readers arrive at this outcome. In fact, close reading is more of a verb than a noun, as much about the journey as it is about the destination. Here's how other educators and professional book authors describe close reading:

From Nancy Frey and Doug Fisher (2013) in their book *Rigorous Reading: 5 Access Points for Comprehending Complex Texts*:

> Close reading is in part about discovering—in this case, discovering what the author meant and how to come to terms with the ideas in the text. (p. 56)

From Kylene Beers and Robert Probst (2013) in *Notice & Note: Strategies for Close Reading*:

> Close reading then should not imply that we ignore the reader's experience and attend closely to the text and nothing else. It should imply that we bring the text and the reader close together. To ignore either element in the transaction, to deny the presence of the reader or neglect the contribution of the text is to make reading impossible. If we understand close reading this way, when the reader is brought into the text we have the opportunity for relevance, engagement, and rigor. (p. 36)

Close reading is more of a verb than a noun, as much about the journey as it is about the destination.

From Laura Robb (2013) in *Unlocking Complex Texts: A Systematic Framework for Building Adolescents' Comprehension*:

> Close reading is a strategy that can help you figure out a difficult word or understand a challenging piece of text. When you're reading a text, assume that every word and phrase carries meaning. If you're unsure of what something means, pause and do a close reading. (p. 262)

From Tim Shanahan (2012) in his blog *Shanahan on Literacy*:

> I think with this brief description of the essentials of close reading (e.g., intense emphasis on text, figuring out the text by thinking about the words and ideas in the text, minimization of external explanations, multiple and dynamic rereading, multiple purposes that focus on what a text says, how it says it, and what it means or what its value is), teachers can start to think clearly about a number of issues in close reading. (para. 6)

Shanahan goes on to elaborate on a number of "issues in close reading"—such as previewing a text and setting a purpose, rereading, and prior knowledge. I, too, will elaborate on these issues in subsequent chapters in this book.

From the PARCC Curriculum Framework:

> Close, analytic reading stresses examining meaning thoroughly and methodically, encouraging students to read and reread deliberately. Directing student attention on the text itself empowers students to understand the central ideas and key supporting details. It also enables students to reflect on the meanings of individual words and sentences; the order in which sentences unfold; and the development of ideas over the course of the text, which ultimately leads students to arrive at an understanding of the text as a whole. (PARCC, 2012, p. 7)

Did you read closely enough to extract the key words from this mosaic of descriptions and definitions? Discovering what the author meant; bringing the text and the reader together; figuring out a difficult word or challenging part of a text; minimizing external explanations; reading for multiple purposes; reading thoroughly and methodically; rereading; attending to the text itself, its central ideas, supporting details, the meaning of individual words and sentences, sentence order, and development of ideas. Notice that in all these definitions of close reading it is the author and the text itself that leads the way, but notice, too, Beers and Probst's (2013) mention of "bringing the text and the reader together." I love that because it positions the reader as central to the process of close reading.

Even at this early stage of CCSS implementation, as a field we are falling into bad old habits of perpetuating misconceptions by taking sides and typecasting old and "new" practices as one thing but *definitely* not the other. For example, with close reading, I fear some educators think it's all about figuring out what the author wrote and that the reader cannot/should not bring much to the party. We need to pause to think about this a little more and reach our own responsible conclusion. Personally, I stand here on the shoulders of Louise Rosenblatt (1938) and her good work so many decades ago in *Literature as Exploration:*

> The reader brings to the work personality traits, memories of past events, present needs and preoccupations, a particular mood of the moment, and a particular physical condition. These and many other elements in a never-to-be-duplicated combination determine his [or her] response to the peculiar contribution of the text. (pp. 30–31)

How can we keep the focus on the author's meaning and at the same time take full advantage of the richness of everything a reader brings to the text?

What this preeminent scholar of literacy would have us recognize is that like it or not, readers bring a great deal of themselves to what they read. So the questions we need to resolve in light of close reading are these: How can we honor both the reader and the text in a more consistently balanced way than we have in the last few decades? How can we keep the focus on the author's meaning and at the same time take full advantage of the richness of everything a reader brings to the text? To answer these questions, we need to examine more closely the instructional best practices that have found their way into our classrooms in recent years. Can we make those *best* practices even *better?* Can we find a niche there in our curriculum for close reading?

Will *All* Reading Be *Close* Reading?

This is a question I get from teachers a lot as I work with them. Absolutely not! There are many kinds of reading we should do with children, and close reading should take its place among them. Think about all the purposes we have when we read. The chart in Figure 1.1, Possible Purposes for Reading, will help to put this into perspective.

Notice that there are many reasons for reading that do not require close reading. There's the read-aloud, just for fun, and I hope we'll never abandon that—for the sake of close reading or for anything else. There are those times when students will simply need to retrieve some basic information. As we've already determined, extracting evidence, though a place to begin for close reading, doesn't meet the close reading criteria as set out by the array of definitions we examined above. When we use that evidence, integrating it to recognize central themes and big ideas in the context of the crafting of a text—*that* is close reading.

But sometimes students need to go even beyond this, the close reading of one text; they need to read *many* texts to fully comprehend an entire body of knowledge. For example, in the chart in Figure 1.1, the goal of interpreting the American dream would be an example of reading for this broader knowledge acquisition goal. So would learning algebra or understanding Renaissance art. Where close reading will fit among this range of reading purposes and how much close reading we will need to do in our classroom will be explained in detail throughout the chapters of this book. To get there, we will need to tweak some of our past practices.

Figure 1.1

Possible Purposes for Reading

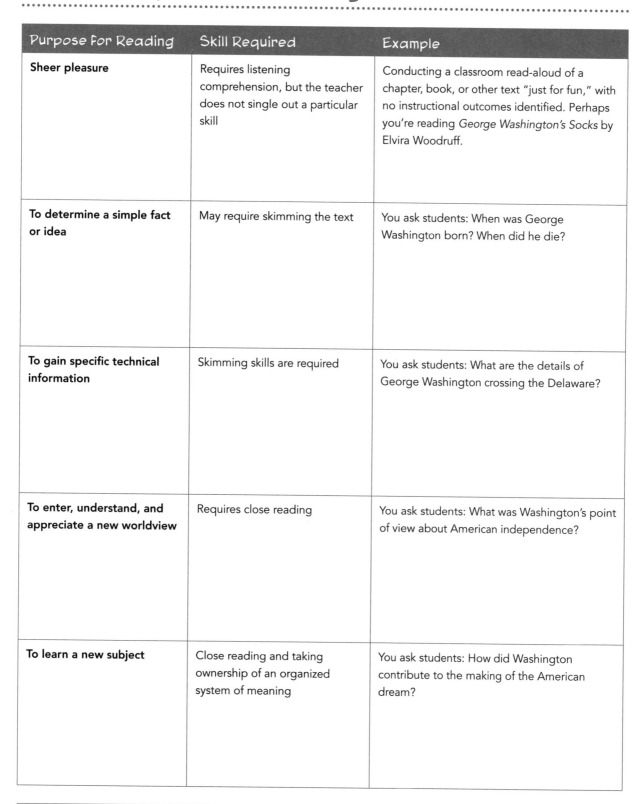

Purpose for Reading	Skill Required	Example
Sheer pleasure	Requires listening comprehension, but the teacher does not single out a particular skill	Conducting a classroom read-aloud of a chapter, book, or other text "just for fun," with no instructional outcomes identified. Perhaps you're reading *George Washington's Socks* by Elvira Woodruff.
To determine a simple fact or idea	May require skimming the text	You ask students: When was George Washington born? When did he die?
To gain specific technical information	Skimming skills are required	You ask students: What are the details of George Washington crossing the Delaware?
To enter, understand, and appreciate a new worldview	Requires close reading	You ask students: What was Washington's point of view about American independence?
To learn a new subject	Close reading and taking ownership of an organized system of meaning	You ask students: How did Washington contribute to the making of the American dream?

Source: Adapted from Paul and Elder (2008).

Tweaking Past Practices

We are implementing many solid, research-supported literacy practices in our classroom. Shout out to teachers: You are doing many things right! With any new initiative (and few initiatives are bigger than the implementation of the CCSS), the intent is not to throw out everything you thought you knew about teaching reading and start over. Your experience and the wisdom you bring to your work are valuable. But there are tweaks we can make. Sometimes it's not the big ideas but the small details that get in the way of students' best performance. Let's take a fresh look at some of these little details within the big ideas and the tweaks that might be in order.

Level of Text Complexity

Over the past several years, teachers have gotten really good at using assessment data to place students in texts at their instructional reading level for reading instruction. We can trace the importance of this all the way back to Vygotsky (1978) and his work on the "zone of proximal development" (ZPD), which helped us understand that students perform best when new learning occurs at that critical juncture of "not too hard, and not too easy." Some "knowledgeable other" (in this case, their teacher) guides them through the challenges they encounter along the way, helping them to achieve success. In fact, the practice we call "guided reading" is built on this premise of working within in a student's "just right"–level ZPD.

But could it be that despite our emphasis on leveled books, we didn't always evaluate whether students were progressing swiftly enough from level to level? Can we admit that maybe sometimes we have not actually been teaching in many of our students' ZPD but, rather, a little beneath it? The Common Core suggests that students need more close encounters with complex texts for optimal growth. We can do this without falling prey to "too hard" texts; helping students deeply comprehend and do complex thinking around texts is central to our goal.

In addition to examining practices around text-to-reader matches, we need to consider the following:

- What makes a text complex?
- How much complex text should students read? While there is general consensus about the definition of complexity, there is decidedly less agreement about how much and how often students should engage with it.
- And above all, how do we guide students through complex text?

Read on. I answer those questions throughout the remainder of this book.

A New Mantra: Teach the Reader *and* the Reading

"Teach the reader, not the reading" has been a mantra of sorts over the past several years. With regard to comprehension, this has generated an emphasis on metacognitive strategies, such as questioning, visualizing, and connecting. There is strong research support for the teaching of strategies. I look especially to the work of Michael Pressley regarding the integrated application of comprehension strategies in a manner that also encourages discourse among teachers and students. His term for this is "transactional strategy instruction" (Pressley et al., 1992).

My book *Constructing Meaning Through Kid-Friendly Strategy Instruction* (Boyles, 2004) exemplifies a "kid-friendly" (as well as *teacher-friendly*) means of bringing comprehension strategy instruction to life in the classroom using this integrated strategy approach. We know from Pressley's research and the research of others, as well as from the work of practitioners such as Harvey and Goudvis (2007), Keene and Zimmermann (2007), and Miller (2013b)—in addition to our own practice—that comprehension strategy instruction can be powerful stuff; we know that teaching students how to be strategic readers truly can lead to deeper thinking.

A couple of tweaks may be important here, too. First, we want to make sure we encourage students to use metacognitive strategies in a way that truly enhances their understanding of the text itself. Over the past few years, metacognition attained a sort of rock star status as the go-to means of improving students' comprehension. Even today as I model lessons in classrooms, sometimes I can barely get through a single sentence of a book without kids' hands flying up: "I have a picture in my mind. . . . I'm wondering. . . . I have a connection."

Based on some of the connections, questions, and visualizations students share, it's clear that these strategy applications do little to uncover the author's intent— especially those sketchy connections: "My dog looks just like that." "Once I fell off my bike, too." It's great when children can relate to the books they read, but these surface-level observations don't begin to approach the way strategies can and should be used to tease out nuances of a text's deeper meaning. Both this chapter and Chapter 8 address the "tweaked" role of metacognitive strategies in more detail.

Coupled with this concern about the superficial use of strategies, I'm also wondering if maybe we've emphasized comprehension strategies, and the cognitive *process*, a bit too much in the intermediate grades, at the expense of using instructional time to understand more about the text itself. When we overfocus on comprehension strategies, we are essentially using the text as a vehicle to understand how text works. Yes, there's a place for this ("teach the reader"). But if we select high-quality resources for our instruction, we should also do our best to bring students to a thorough understanding of all the meaning that book (or news article or other source) has to offer. Maybe our new mantra should be this: "Teach the reader *and* the reading." That is very much in line with the way we have defined close reading above, the CCSS themselves, and the instructional model described in depth in the chapters that follow this one.

Scaffolding Literacy Learning

For sound instructional practices, I look also to the work of P. David Pearson and Margaret C. Gallagher (1983) and their model of explicit instruction (sometimes referred to as *I do, we do, you do*), gradually releasing responsibility from the teacher to the student until the student has achieved independence. In this model, there are four levels of support:

1. **I do, you watch:** Instruction begins with an explanation and modeling where the teacher has the lion's share of control over the learning process, clearly articulating a few basic steps to meet success with the lesson objective and modeling the way this would look in action. For example, if the objective is summarizing a story, the teacher would identify what goes into a good summary and then show students how he or she might go about writing a summary based on the fairy tale *The Three Little Pigs*.

2. **I do, you help:** In this instructional phase, students begin to take on some responsibility for the learning themselves, with the teacher asking for input from them at strategic points in the lesson. Using another fairy tale, perhaps *Little Red Riding Hood*, the teacher may ask, "What should we include in our summary from the *beginning* of the story?" This would require students to take into account and incorporate the summary criteria that their teacher had previously explained and modeled.

3. **You do, I help:** Now the balance of power shifts. The teacher steps back and lets students take on most of the control for learning themselves, but the teacher is poised to jump in with support when needed. Here, students may use a graphic organizer to guide their summary. Or maybe the teacher offers some verbal support: "I like the way you included the characters at the beginning of your summary. But what about the problem? Could you include a sentence about that, too?"

4. **You do, I watch:** In this final instructional stage, the students have all the control, and the teacher simply looks on. At this point, students are independent in their application of the skill or strategy and are ready for assessment. They may be tasked with writing a summary for a fairy tale or other problem-solution story entirely on their own—no teacher input allowed.

Although this is a four-phase process, that does not mean there will need to be only four lessons for all students to reach independence. Some students will move efficiently through the gradual release of responsibility while others will stall at one stage or another, requiring an even more gradual transition to independent mastery.

If I had to choose one principle that has influenced my teaching more than any other, it would be this one, the gradual release of responsibility model. It is essential to students' success as readers that we systematically move them not just to mastery of a skill, but to independent application of that skill even when the teacher is not there to support them.

Still, I pause to reflect on the way this model has sometimes been implemented in reading instruction. Focusing on a specific skill or strategy has often meant that on a given day, students set their sights exclusively on a single aspect of a text (its main idea, author's purpose, passages to visualize, and the like) and look only for places within their reading that provide such evidence. Over several days, returning to that skill or strategy in multiple texts helps students become more independent in its use.

But does this approach help students develop a deeper understanding of the text as a whole? Understanding individual elements of a text in the context of the *entire* work is a key feature of close reading and an adjustment we will want to make to our teaching of literacy if students are to gain maximum benefit from our instruction.

What impact might a wisely implemented gradual release model have on our comprehension strategy instruction? Where will the metacognitive strategies fit within a comprehensive model of close reading instruction? And most important of all, how will we apply this gradual-release model to close reading in order to scaffold students effectively? There is so much we need to learn about instructional scaffolding in light of Common Core expectations. Subsequent chapters explore in depth the way we support readers before, during, and after close reading. But before moving on to this analysis, let's put all of this together into an instructional model that captures close reading the way it will be described in this book.

Recommended Resources on Close Reading

There are lots of ways to move forward with close reading. The path I have chosen for this book works well for elementary-grade students just learning the art of close reading. It is based on a systematic, explicit model of scaffolded instruction that guides young students (and their teachers) through the reading process step-by-step. But there are other ways of being "systematic" and "explicit" that can also support the navigation of complex text.

Two professional books that are similar in scope, but somewhat different in their approach, are Laura Robb's (2013) *Unlocking Complex Texts: A Systematic Framework for Building Adolescents' Comprehension* and Nancy Frey and Doug Fisher's (2013) *Rigorous Reading: 5 Access Points for Comprehending Complex Text.*

Laura Robb (2013) organizes her book around genres: biography, memoir, myths, short stories, texts that argue, and poetry. In addition to the appendix, which contains assorted classroom-ready materials, the accompanying CD is like unwrapping a gift. There's a file for each genre, with book lists for differentiation, skill-building task sheets, and best of all, the short texts themselves—several of them for each genre.

The Frey and Fisher book (2013) identifies five means of accessing complex texts. In addition to close reading, which is one of the access points, these authors include purpose and modeling, collaborative conversation, independent reading, demonstrating understanding, and assessing performance. This book includes six modules for professional development, with PowerPoint slides to bring these access points to life.

The Instructional Model

Teaching Close Reading in a Ninety-Minute Literacy Block

The graphics that follow will go a long way to help you envision how close reading fits in with what you already do. These charts provide a bird's-eye view of the model of close reading that I lay out in the course of this book.

Figure 1.2

When You Introduce a Complex Text During an *Initial* Close Reading Lesson

How the Literacy Block Supports Deep Understanding of Content

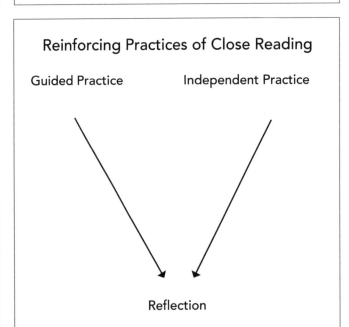

NINETY MINUTES

SHARED READING

GUIDED, INDEPENDENT, REFLECTION

Getting Ready for Close Reading	3 to 5 Minutes
Get students to focus	
Identify your purpose	
Activate strategies for accessing the text	

Building Text Understanding Through Close Reading	20 to 25 Minutes
Ask text-dependent questions	
Model as necessary	
Build strategies for independent close reading	

Reinforcing Practices of Close Reading

Guided Practice   Independent Practice

Reflection

60 Minutes

Figure 1.3

When You Reread a Complex Text During a *Follow-Up* Close Reading Lesson

How the Literacy Block Supports the Reinforcement of Comprehension Skills and Strategies

NINETY MINUTES	**SHARED READING**	**Getting Ready for Rereading** Get students to focus Review and link Identify an objective	3 to 5 Minutes
		Building a Reading Skill or Strategy Explain ↓ Model ↓ Release to greater independence	10 to 20 Minutes
	GUIDED, INDEPENDENT, REFLECTION	**Reinforcing Reading Skills and Strategies** Guided Practice Independent Practice ↘ ↙ Reflection	60 to 70 Minutes

Available for download at **www.corwin.com/closerreading**

Like any sound instructional model, this reading model represents how the key touchstone practices build together. The assumptions at work are as follows:

- All practices align with the idea that a close reading must prominently feature the text itself, while also recognizing the uniqueness of each reader.

- Complex texts are those that yield rigorous, engaged reading and discussion; they have sufficient heft of ideas and content in terms of their craft and structure, thematic and emotional power, and important informational and conceptual understandings.

- Comprehension strategies and skills are modeled and practiced thoughtfully but are addressed in the context of—and in tandem with—comprehending the content; they are applied as a means of understanding the text rather than as an end in themselves.

- Instructional scaffolding that adheres to the gradual release of responsibility model is preferable to teacher-centric lessons and demonstrations in which the burden of comprehension is on the teacher rather than on the students; moving students toward independence is of paramount importance.

To capture all these operating beliefs about teaching and learning, I offer the above two graphics to reflect that we have *two* responsibilities to readers:

1. We need to help them understand the content of a *particular* text (see Figure 1.2, When You Introduce a Complex Text During an *Initial* Close Reading Lesson: How the Literacy Block Supports Deep Understanding of Content).

2. We need to simultaneously move them forward as strategic thinkers about *any* text (see Figure 1.3, When You Reread a Complex Text During a *Follow-Up* Close Reading Lesson: How the Literacy Block Supports the Reinforcement of Skills and Strategies).

I love visual representations such as these because they provide an at-a-glance view of the big picture. The trouble is that it's hard to know where to focus first in order to make sense of the components individually and then figure out how they work together. Multiply that times two in this case because there are two graphics. We'll look first at the similarities between an initial close reading lesson and a follow-up lesson, and then we'll examine their differences.

The Initial Lesson and the Follow-Up Rereading Lesson: How They Are Alike

The two graphics (Figure 1.2 and Figure 1.3) have been placed side by side to make it easier for you to examine them comparatively. First, the similarities: Your very first observation may be the words in extra-large, bold font: NINETY MINUTES. "Oh, no," you may be thinking, "I'm already in trouble. I don't have a ninety-minute literacy block." If this is your situation, know that many teachers with whom I work face this same issue. It just makes sense that if we have more time on task and use the time well, we can accomplish more. But even if you have only an hour or forty-five minutes, you can still make this plan work. Try to protect your minutes for an initial shared (whole-class) close reading lesson since that's where new ways of thinking about text will be introduced. Time for small-group instruction and independent reading is crucial too since that's where students practice what they have learned. If you must shave minutes, consider doing fewer follow-up strategy and skill-based close reading lessons. This means that for a given text you will need to be more selective about specific complexities of a text that you address, though over time you can find opportunities for highlighting many critical textual elements.

Another common feature of both graphics is the consistent inclusion of three instructional formats: *shared, guided,* and *independent* reading as well as *reflection.* This provides balance throughout the literacy block, helping us meet students' individual learning needs through multiple grouping options. Notice, too, the three consistent instructional components: *Getting Ready, Building,* and *Reinforcing.* You'll want to take a closer look at exactly what is included under each of these three headings since that's where these images diverge, along with the instruction for both kinds of lessons—an initial close reading lesson and a follow-up lesson to build a skill or strategy through rereading a text.

Before exploring this difference, however, there is a consistent aspect of the *Reinforcing* component of the model for both an introductory close reading lesson and a follow-up lesson that teachers find helpful. I call it my "20–20–20 plan." This is where we differentiate our instruction. The idea is that within the hour devoted to reinforcing literacy learning, students spend twenty minutes reading independently, twenty minutes in a small group guided by their teacher, and twenty minutes engaged in some kind of follow-up application of their learning from the whole-class or small-group lesson. This application might be responding in a reading journal, writing an answer to an open-ended question, collaborating with a partner or a couple of peers on a literacy task, or just about anything that reinforces their comprehension. While students are engaged in this three-way rotation, the teacher is available to work with three groups.

The Initial Lesson and the Follow-Up Rereading Lesson: How They Are Different

While we always want to prepare students for reading, there will be marked differences between the way we've done this in the past and the manner suggested for close reading with the Common Core in mind. We will make a further distinction between preparing for an initial close reading lesson aimed at a broad *purpose* and a follow-up close reading most likely directed toward a more specific, focused *objective.*

The Initial Reading. The purpose of the reading itself (as always) is to build understanding, though what we're building *toward* will vary from an initial close reading to rereading. The first time around, we will seek understanding of the broad meaning of the text itself, both content and craft, through teacher-led, text-dependent questions coupled with strategies to help students construct meaning independently.

The Second Reading. In this model, rereading a second time (and possibly additional rereadings beyond that) will work toward skill and strategy development through systematic, explicit teaching that gradually releases responsibility from teacher to students.

Small-Group and Independent Practice. Small-group (guided) instruction and independent reading will remain important parts of our literacy block and will serve, just as in the past, to reinforce literacy learning. Now there will be two options: (a) reinforcing understanding of the content and craft of a text to develop a deeper understanding of its particular complexities or (b) using a text as a means to reinforce the application of skills and strategies so students may transfer them to the study of *any* text.

Reflection Time. Notice on both graphics that our literacy block closes with a time for students to reflect on their learning. This is hardly a new idea, though too often rather than thoughtful conversation about insights into the reading process, the end of the literacy block is actually signaled by the ringing of the lunch bell or some other arbitrary division between reading and whatever comes next in the school day. For even more reinforcement of close reading we should challenge ourselves to carry meaning making into the final few minutes of the time we devote to reading each day.

Onward Into Closer Reading

For a little more elaboration on each of the two graphics (Figures 1.2 and 1.3), see the next two charts—Figure 1.4, When You Introduce a Complex Text During an *Initial* Close Reading Lesson: Understanding the Focus on Deep Understanding of Content, and Figure 1.5, When You Reread a Complex Text During a *Follow-Up* Close Reading Lesson: Understanding the Focus on Reinforcing Comprehension Skills and Strategies. These charts explain in more detail the range of instructional formats, types of text appropriate for each component of instruction, approximate number of minutes for and the purpose of each instructional format in light of close reading, and probable teaching practices. Think of these charts as a preview of *what* you will learn in Chapters 2 through 9 of this book. These chapters will also show you *how*— that is, how to plan and implement the best possible close reading instruction.

Each chapter zooms in on one aspect of close reading, showing you exactly how that will look in an intermediate-grade classroom—both the planning and the implementation. Here's what you can expect:

- Chapter 2. Choosing a Complex Text for Close Reading
- Chapter 3. Getting in the Mindset of Close Reading
- Chapter 4. Supporting Readers *Before* Close Reading
- Chapter 5. Supporting Readers *During* Close Reading
- Chapter 6. Supporting Readers *After* Close Reading
- Chapter 7. Moving Students Toward Independence in Close Reading

Format	Text	Minutes	Purpose	Instructional Practices
Independent reading with easier texts that involve at least some intellectual challenge	Literary or informational texts Encourage the use of longer texts to build stamina, though shorter texts may also be included.	About 60 minutes (concurrent with small-group instruction and/or conferring)	Reinforce practices of close reading and skills and strategies aligned to standards and students' data-driven literacy needs using texts that students can read on their own.	Reading for stamina and enjoyment with *some* attention to practices of close reading and reinforcement of individual skills and strategies. May include individual or partner reading, literature circles, or technology-enhanced literacy experiences such as use of electronic readers, video, and online sources.
Reflecting on reading	Will probably focus on texts used for independent reading	About 5 to 10 minutes	Reflect on new learning about the practices of close reading for deep understanding.	Share evidence within independent reading text where close reading practices have been applied.

 Available for download at **www.corwin.com/closerreading**

Figure 1.5

When You Reread a Complex Text During a *Follow-Up* Close Reading Lesson

Understanding the Focus on Reinforcing Comprehension Skills and Strategies

Format	Text	Minutes	Purpose	Instructional Practices
Whole-class (shared) rereading with complex text	The same literary or informational text used for the initial close reading lesson	About 10 to 20 minutes	Close rereading *can* be general, rereading a whole text for deeper meaning, but will more likely focus on places within a text that reinforce a particular skill (like identifying an author's purpose) or lead to better application of a metacognitive strategy (such as visualizing descriptive paragraphs).	**Before reading:** Review key ideas from the introductory close reading of the text; link to current follow-up lesson; identify objective and criteria for success. **During reading:** Explain how to approach the objective strategically; model the application of the skill or strategy; gradually release students to more independent application of the skill or strategy. **After reading:** Provide opportunities for skill or strategy follow-up tasks that feature collaboration with peers and oral response before written response (may occur on a subsequent day depending on time).
Small-group (guided) reading or conferring with "stretch" instructional level texts	Literary or informational texts Passages from longer texts such as chapter books, short informational sources on nonfiction topics, or literary texts such as short stories or poems	About 60 minutes (concurrent with independent reading)	Reinforce practices of close reading and skills and strategies aligned to standards and students' data-driven literacy needs using texts that students can read with teacher support. Texts may offer a bit more intellectual challenge than instructional level texts used in the past.	Differentiated scaffolding for different learners may occur in small-group instruction or through conferences with individual students. Instruction may focus on practices of close reading for deep textual understanding or reinforcement of specific skills and strategies.

Format	Text	Minutes	Purpose	Instructional Practices
Independent reading with easier texts that involve at least some intellectual challenge	Range of literary or informational texts of different genres Encourage the use of longer texts to build stamina, though shorter texts may also be included.	About 60 minutes (concurrent with small-group instruction and/or conferring)	Reinforce practices of close reading and skills and strategies aligned to standards and students' data-driven literacy needs using texts that students can read on their own.	Reading for stamina and enjoyment with *some* attention to practices of close reading and reinforcement of specific skills and strategies. May include individual or partner reading, literature circles, or technology-enhanced literacy experiences such as use of electronic readers, video, and online sources.
Reflecting on reading	Will probably focus on texts used for independent reading	About 5 to 10 minutes	Reflect on new learning about the reading *process*.	Share evidence within independent reading text where skill/strategy has been applied.

Available for download at **www.corwin.com/closerreading**

Reflecting on What We Know

1. Think about the population of students in your classroom or in your school. If they continue progressing at their current rate, what percentage of them do you think will be ready for credit-bearing college courses by the time they leave high school? Discuss your thinking.

2. In what ways has this chapter changed or clarified your understanding of what you *thought* close reading to be?

3. Discuss to what extent you think your current literacy program or curriculum supports close reading. What is the evidence?

4. This chapter identified a few past practices we might want to tweak to better align with close reading for the Common Core: the level of text complexity, balancing a focus on skills and strategies with a focus on content, and the way we scaffold instruction. What are your thoughts on these tweaks? Are there any other tweaks that come to mind?

5. What aspects of the model for a ninety-minute literacy block, shown in Figures 1.2 and 1.3, resonated with you? Look closely at one part of the graphic or chart and consider its implications for your classroom.

6. What else do you need to know about close reading in order to move forward with it? What questions do you hope the remainder of this book will answer?

Choosing a Complex Text for Close Reading

Instructional Shift

Before the Common Core Skill or Strategy Lessons	With the Common Core Close Reading Lessons
The Text: The text selected for the lesson was at most students' instructional level; it was a text students couldn't necessarily read on their own but could read with teacher support. It was chosen to address students' skill or strategy needs but not especially for its complexity of ideas or structural complexity. The texts tended to be whole texts, called anchor texts or touchstone texts, and were often used to introduce or practice a reading strategy or a specific skill.	**The Text:** The text for a close reading lesson is selected for its complexity first and foremost; the expert teacher knows that it will represent significant challenge to all students and require significant guidance from the teacher to support students' full comprehension. The text may be complex in content, theme, ideas, or inference load but written in short, simple sentences. Conversely, it may have complex sentence structures and vocabulary but have accessible content and ideas. The texts tend to be shorter: picture books, articles, chapter openings, or passages.

The Instructional Shift

The first order of business when planning a close reading lesson is to find a good text—more specifically, a good *complex* text. Complex doesn't necessarily mean the text is long or has obtuse, rococo sentences. The text can have short, simple sentences, but something about it is complex and challenging—for example, abstract ideas requiring the reader to make a lot of inferences, dialogue between characters that is confusing in some way, complex historical content that is full of new vocabulary, or multiple points of view represented within the piece, where one or more perspectives are outside students' range of experiences. The important thing is you want to choose a text that is rich enough so that students can, with your help, mine it for *all* its meaning, thereby advancing their capacity to think deeply about what they read.

Common Core Components of Text Complexity

The Common Core gives us guidance about text complexity in Appendix A, making it clear that using complex text for close reading is nonnegotiable, contingent on three factors:

1. Quantitative assessment of the text

2. Qualitative features of the text

3. Reader and task considerations (National Governers Association, 2010a, p. 4)

Quantitative Complexity

Quantitative complexity is measured by Lexile, essentially a readability score based on sentence length and word frequency. Note that "word frequency" does not mean the number of times a word appears in *this* particular text but, rather, is a mathematical estimate of its likelihood to appear in *any* text. You will note in Table 2.1 that the Common Core recommends that students read at significantly higher Lexiles at much earlier grade levels.

To appreciate the full impact of this call for higher expectations of readers, note that the upper Lexile limit for Grade 8 in the past was 1010. With the advent of the Common Core and an update in 2012 to reflect additional research, 1010 is now at the top of the range for Grade 5. In other words, students will be expected to read text at this complexity level three years earlier! Note the marked upward trend in Lexiles for other grades, too.

Qualitative Complexity

Remember that Lexile is only *one* consideration in gauging a text's difficulty. We should never toss aside a text just because its Lexile is outside the prescribed

Remember that Lexile is only one consideration in gauging a text's difficulty. We should never toss aside a text just because its Lexile is outside the prescribed grade range.

Table 2.1

Grade Band	Lexile Band Before the Common Core	"Stretch" Lexile Band
K–1	N/A	N/A
2–3	450L–725L	420L–820L
4–5	645L–845L	740L–1010L
6–8	860L–1010L	925L–1185L
9–10	960L–1115L	1050L–1335L
11–CCR[a]	1070L–1220L	1185L–1385L

Source: Text Complexity Grade Bands and Lexile Bands (2013).

a. CCR = college and career readiness.

grade range. Most important to me in selecting a text are the text's qualitative complexities. Appendix A of the Common Core cites four broad *qualitative* areas to examine (National Governors Association, 2010a):

1. *Knowledge demands* consider what readers are likely to bring to the table in terms of background knowledge compared to what knowledge the text expects the reader to have to comprehend it. *What background knowledge is "demanded" by this text?*

2. *Meaning* refers to those aspects of a text related to the author's message, such as the amount of inferential thinking required, sophistication of its themes, amount of information included, and number of diverse perspectives represented.

3. *Language* becomes complex when there are many unknown words or when the images are figurative rather than literal.

4. *Text structure* can also account for increased complexity when there are multiple structures or multiple narrators, or when the structure is not a simple sequence of events.

These four criteria are further delineated in the chart in Figure 2.1. Use this chart yourself or with colleagues to identify more specifically what makes a particular text complex. I try to find texts that are complex (designated by a rating of "3") in two or three areas. A few other criteria on the chart may warrant a rating of "2," and it's fine to have some other text components that are not really complex at all, earning a rating of "1." Choosing text that is complex in too many of the areas cited in the chart will lead to confusion for students, not comprehension.

Figure 2.1

Is This Text Complex?

Title of text: _____   **Author:** _____

Quantitative Text Features

Lexile level for books (www.scholastic.com/bookwizard):

Qualitative Text Features

Criteria	Very Complex 3	Somewhat Complex 2	Not Complex 1	Comments
Knowledge demands				
Connection to a student's life experiences, culture, literary or subject area knowledge vs. no connections				
Few allusions to other texts vs. many allusions (intertextuality)				
Meaning				
Single theme vs. multiple themes				
Simple theme vs. complex theme				
Perspective similar to one's own vs. unlike/opposite perspective				
Single perspective vs. multiple perspectives				
Mostly literal-level thinking required vs. many inferences				
Language				
Straightforward language vs. sophisticated language (imagery, figurative language, etc.)				

Criteria	Very Complex 3	Somewhat Complex 2	Not Complex 1	Comments
Mostly familiar words vs. many new/unknown words				
Short, simple sentences vs. long, complicated sentences				
Text structure				
Simple sequential structure vs. complex nonlinear structure				
Supporting illustrations, subheadings, and so on vs. no helpful graphics or text features				

Task Features and Context

Students will demonstrate their understanding of this text by:

These students probably do/do not have the necessary background knowledge for this text.

Rating

As an overall assessment for <u>these students</u>, I would rate this text:

___ very complex   ___ somewhat complex   ___ not complex

because:

As practicing teachers, you already have an intuitive sense of literary and informational texts that offer enough challenge to yield effective lessons; conversely, you know when a text is too hard. So don't be intimidated by the Common Core's three complexity factors—quantitative assessment of the text, qualitative features of the text, and reader and task considerations—and don't think you need to evaluate texts with utmost accuracy. That said, becoming familiar with the full range of qualitative complexities specified by the Common Core will help you choose complex texts more knowledgeably.

Reader and Task Considerations

The third and final component of text complexity that the Common Core identifies is *reader and task considerations*. The previous two factors, defining quantitative and qualitative dimensions of a text, are intended to be more generic, applying to *all* readers at a particular grade level who would engage with an identified text. This final factor, by comparison, has more to do with the readers in *your* class: What motivates *them*? How has *their* previous experience with classic poetry or a story told in verse, for example, contributed to their perception about the next text you hand them for close reading? Do you have a lot of special needs students? English language learners? Students who are reluctant to take risks as readers? Students who can't sit still for more than ten minutes? We need to factor in these considerations, too, when choosing texts for close reading.

We also need to think about how students will be expected to respond to the texts they read (National Governors Association, 2010a). If the task we plan for a particular close reading lesson will require responses to fairly straightforward questions without much higher-level thinking or application of knowledge, the text can be quite challenging. If thoughtful, open-ended questions will be asked that tap inference and analysis of a single selection, maybe a more moderate level of complexity is in order. If multiple texts must be digested and synthesized, with ideas integrated into a full-length story or essay, the reading will likely need to be easier still.

Finding the *Best* Complex Texts

"But where do you *find* all these great books?" Teachers ask me this question all the time. And while it's useful to know what the Common Core considers complex, it hardly guarantees that the text you choose for today's lesson is going to be a smashing success. It's ultimately up to you to immerse yourself in knowing children's literature inside and out—and fortunately, there are plenty of places to turn to for guidance (see Appendix IV, page 188, for a list of websites and pages 32–35 for my favorites).

I have to confess here that I am pretty much addicted to children's literature. It's my guilty, geeky pleasure. I always bring a suitcase of books to workshops, and in return teachers tell me about their favorites. The upshot is that my Amazon cart is consistently full to overflowing. (They actually offered me an installment plan recently to empty my shopping cart and pay up!)

How do I decide which texts to select? I *love* picture books for close reading. They can usually be read in a single sitting, they offer interesting characters or real-life people (even animals) working through critical situations, and they lead to an important message—all within thirty-two pages, with the added bonus of magnificent illustrations to support the words.

Texts that appeal to me and to students in intermediate elementary grades and that are meaty enough for rigorous discussion and analysis incorporate the following elements:

- Topics beyond students' everyday experiences and comfort zone that offer the opportunity to examine injustice and challenges: the Holocaust, immigration, civil rights, slavery, racial profiling, homelessness, and so on

- Common kid problems handled in unique ways that don't necessarily lead to "Disney endings"

- Situations that feature multicultural characters in authentic ways, especially Middle Eastern characters (which are hard to find)

- Characters/people who persevere in the face of obstacles or hardships in order to achieve their dreams

- Character studies where you learn a lot about a character's or person's values and what motivates him or her

- Turning points that are open to interpretation (not clear-cut)

- Poetic language that creates vivid images

- First-person narratives with strong voice (especially when the "voice" doesn't really talk—like the story is told from a goldfish's point of view or from the standpoint of a tree or garbage truck)

- Alternate voices—like hearing the story of *Cinderella* from her stepmother's point of view

- Informational texts that demonstrate a range of writers' crafts and word choice that evokes powerful images—such as books by Nicola Davies, Robert Burleigh, and Judith St. George

- Science and history books in which photographs take center stage (great opportunities for examining primary sources)

Every teacher has his or her own short list of authors whose work strikes a chord with their students and lends itself to instruction, and it's important to find your own way. But if you want examples of authors I consider "close reading caliber" I recommend just about anything by Cynthia Rylant, Eve Bunting, and Jacqueline Woodson. To accommodate the Common Core's emphasis on short texts for close reading, I also track down worthy short stories, poems, informational articles, and

(Text continued on page 36)

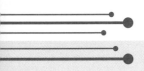

Absolute Favorite Close Reading Texts
for the Intermediate Grades

Narrative Picture Books

More Than Anything Else by Marie Bradby: A story about Booker T. Washington's childhood; he wanted to read "more than anything else" and pursued this dream against great odds; lots of inferences; told from Booker's point of view. (Grades 3–5)

Mercedes and the Chocolate Pilot by Margot Theis Raven: A true story of a young German girl's unique friendship with Lt. Gail Halvorsen in post-World War II Berlin; great message; bring tissues . . . This one gets me every time. (Grades 4–6)

The Raft by Jim LaMarche: Feels a bit like *Tom Sawyer*; excellent first-person narrative; lots of opportunities to consider another point of view (Grandma's); well crafted; good for identifying words that contribute to tone. (Grades 3–5)

Testing the Ice: A True Story of Jackie Robinson by Sharon Robinson: First-person story about Jackie Robinson told by his daughter; leads to serious inferential thinking around the double meaning of "testing the ice"—literal and figurative; perhaps my current first choice for close reading. (Grades 3–6)

Each Kindness by Jacqueline Woodson: Amazing story that revolves around some mean girls' exclusion of a student new to their classroom; packs a punch. Sometimes you just don't get a second chance, so consider the feelings of others the *first* time around. (Grades 2–4)

Freedom Summer by Deborah Wiles: The story is set in the South during the civil rights era. Two boys (one black, the other white) are fast friends but must endure the indignity of prejudice and discrimination in ways that will nearly take your breath away—intensified by incredible illustrations with much emotional impact. (Grades 3–6)

One Tiny Turtle by Nicola Davies: A beautifully written nonfiction narrative about the life of a loggerhead turtle; great similes, descriptive language, and a subtext with additional details for even deeper reading. Nicola Davies is my go-to author for informational text rich in craft. (Grades 2–5)

Down the Road by Alice Schertle: A growing-up tale about a little girl who wants to show she can handle responsibility—with not-so-great results; good craft. A standout feature of this book to me is the message about parenting. (Grades 2–4)

Weslandia by Paul Fleischman: This book is perfect for older students who think they're too cool for picture books (they'll be hooked immediately!); wry humor; addresses important issues of adolescence: resisting peer pressure, resourcefulness, creative thinking. Great vocabulary, too. (Grades 4–6)

One Green Apple by Eve Bunting: The story features a Middle-Eastern child new to this country as she struggles with learning English and finding acceptance among her peers. English language learners will relate. There's also the symbolism of the green apple. (Grades 3–5)

14 Cows for America by Carmen Agra Deedy: This is a 9/11 story set among the Maasai tribe in Kenya—replete with the most amazing illustrations you can imagine; incredible message derived from the final sentences and a painting depicting the twin towers reflected in the eyes of a tribesman. (Grades 5–6)

Informational Non-Narrative Picture Books

Ubiquitous by Joyce Sidman: Science facts about a dozen of nature's survivors, such as the gecko and the shark, are paired with poems about these same natural phenomena. Diverse poetic structures create vivid images of each species. Remarkable illustrations, too. Great for text-to-text connections using multiple text formats. Also check out other poetry books about nature from this same author. (Grades 3-6)

Abe's Honest Words by Doreen Rappaport: While this text is written in prose, the appeal to me is its inclusion of direct quotes from Lincoln's speeches to support key moments in his life. What a great way to show students the connection between the man and the values that governed his life. What a wonderful means of introducing young children to the power of primary source material. (Grades 3-6)

Faces of the Moon and *Moon Gazer's Wheel* by Bob Crelin: This book describes the phases of the moon in verse that presents enough content to be meaningful but not so much that students are overwhelmed. Interesting text features include tabs and cut-out illustrations of each phase. The accompanying *Moon Gazer's Wheel* is a fun nontraditional text format for hands-on application. (Grades 2-5)

If the World Were a Village by David Smith: If the world were a village of one hundred people, how many of those people would speak each language, would subscribe to various religions, would have access to clean water or an education? This book examines elements of culture with statistics that is kid-friendly . . . actually, kid-fascinating! (Grades 4-6)

My Secret Camera: Life in the Lodz Ghetto, photographs by Mendel Grossman, text by Frank Dabba Smith: This book is essentially a photo album of life in a concentration camp with pictures taken in secret by a photographer imprisoned in this ghetto. The black-and-white photos captioned by Grossman tell a story more powerful than words alone could possibly impart. Students will long remember the faces of those whose eyes peer from these pages. (Grades 4-6)

Oh, Freedom! Kids Talk About the Civil Rights Movement With the People Who Made It Happen by Casey King and Linda Osborne: Interviews conducted by Washington, D.C., fourth graders with their parents, grandparents, and others who experienced the civil rights movement firsthand show the dedication of ordinary people in the effort to win equal rights for all Americans. Includes iconic photos symbolic of the 1960s. This is a primary source that even young students will understand and appreciate. (Grades 3-6)

At Ellis Island: A History in Many Voices by Louise Peacock: A fictional story is integrated with original sources—quotes and photographs—to help students build an understanding of the challenges faced by children who immigrated to America. Interesting text format with many opportunities for discussion. (Grades 4-6)

Poems

"The Ballad of Birmingham" by Dudley Randall: Told in verse, this is the sad but true story of the Birmingham church bombing in 1963; certainly not a happy ending, but an important moment in American history for students to understand; well crafted with two points of view represented through dialogue. (Grades 4–6)

"Mother to Son" by Langston Hughes: This poem written in dialect is told from the mom's point of view: "Life for me ain't been no crystal stair"; perfect example of an extended metaphor. This poem is a hit every time. (Grades 4–6)

"Coke Bottle Brown" from *Meet Danitra Brown* and "Class Bully" from *My Man Blue* both by Nikki Grimes: These poems work well together for text-to-text connections around bullying; good use of language; emphasize thematic subtleties. (Grades 3–5)

"Autumn" by Emily Dickinson: Although Emily Dickinson might not be the first poet who comes to mind for elementary grade students, this poem works well (and is suggested for Grade 3 in Common Core Appendix B; National Governors Association, 2010b); lots of personification; a few archaic words; useful for learning to paraphrase. (Grades 3–5)

"Golden Keys" by Fred Newtown Scott and Gordon A. Southworth: This is one of the sample stimulus passages identified by the Smarter Balanced Assessment Consortium (SBAC) for Grade 4 (http://www .ode.state.or.us/wma/teachlearn/commoncore/ela-05-cr-1-06-040-v1.pdf). It's another good example of an extended metaphor: describes keys to polite behavior. (Grades 3–5)

"I Hear America Singing" by Walt Whitman and "I, Too, Sing America" by Langston Hughes: The Whitman poem depicts the burgeoning of nineteenth-century middle-class America through hard work and opportunity; the Hughes poem, a response to Whitman, illustrates the concurrent disenfranchisement of African Americans; great companion texts. (Grades 4–6)

"Abraham Lincoln" by Berton Bellis: There's lots of complex vocabulary and many sophisticated concepts to explore in this poem; excellent text to use when students already have a basic understanding of Lincoln. (Grades 5–6)

"The Birthday of Madeline Blore" by Karla Kuskin from *Birthday Surprises* edited by Johanna Hurwitz: This poem, appropriate for younger students, offers up some great imagery and opportunities for inferential thinking. I remove the last line and let the students infer the outcome for themselves; there's ample textual evidence for them to justify their conclusion about Madeline's fate. (Grades 2–4)

"The Library Card" from *My Name Is Jorge: On Both Sides of the River* by Jane Medina: This free-verse poem about a migrant mother and her son includes use of repeated lines for emphasis and a theme that revolves around present-day discrimination; also includes some words in Spanish. (Grades 4–6)

Short Stories

"Spaghetti" from *Every Living Thing* by Cynthia Rylant: This amazing short story features a complex character and his relationship with a kitten he finds. This is probably my very favorite short story. (Grades 4–6)

"Stray" from *Every Living Thing* by Cynthia Rylant: This short story shows the varying perspectives of family members when the daughter brings home a stray cat; clearly defined turning point; heartwarming. (Grades 3–5)

"Eleven" from *Woman Hollering Creek: And Other Stories* by Sandra Cisneros: This is a powerful story of personal angst faced by an early adolescent; excellent character study. (Grades 5–7)

"Five Dollars" from *Hey World, Here I Am!* by Jean Little: This text is only a paragraph long but generates lengthy conversations; so many questions surface here about personal responsibility, what is right and what is wrong—with plenty of opportunities to return to the text for evidence. (Grades 3–5)

"The Mouse at the Seashore" from *Fables* by Arnold Lobel: This is a short, modern fable about taking risks to achieve your dreams. A complicating factor here is that the mouse disobeys his parents en route to reaching his goal—which you might want to know up front before using this story with younger readers. (Grades 3–5)

"My Name is Osama" by Sharifa Alkhateeb and Steven S. Lapham, retrieved from http://www .cga.ct.gov/coc/PDFs/bullying/102107_bullying_myname.pdf: This is an incredible story about racial profiling centering on a young Iraqi boy. It will stir many emotions and generate much conversation; appropriate for more mature readers. (Grades 5–7)

"Secrets of the Shelter" from *Soul Moon Soup* by Phoebe Rose: This is a first-person account from a child who lived in a homeless shelter. The narrator shares insights that could only come from someone who has "been there"; powerful in its simplicity. (Grades 5–7)

"The Fun They Had" by Isaac Asimov, retrieved from http://staff.fcps.net/tcarr/shortstory/fun.htm: This story is a science fiction view of education in the future—where books are a rare, almost unidentifiable commodity and the main characters reflect wistfully on tales they've heard about schools of days gone by. (Grades 4–6)

(Text continued from page 31)

When indentifying complex text for upper-elementary students, make sure "complex" doesn't mean the content is conceptually beyond what is appropriate for preadolescents.

excerpts. Although I'm not a big fan of excerpts in general, I now try to use these within close reading lessons, too; the Common Core assessment consortia draw heavily on brief segments from longer works for their sample test items. We need to teach students how to make sense of a text when they only have a piece of it.

A list of websites that supply short texts useful at various grade levels is available in Appendix IV (and on the book's website at **www.corwin.com/closerreading**). New sites seem to pop up every day, so stay attuned to all that the Internet has to offer. In Appendix V (and at **www.corwin.com/closerreading**), you'll find a bibliography citing hundreds of picture book titles well suited to close reading. They are categorized according to Common Core reading standards. While you will be able to address numerous standards through the close study of any text, the designated standard indicates that a particular text is especially well suited to *this* standard. The aim of the identified standard may be an excellent place to begin when you and your students return to the text for more focused analysis during a follow-up close reading. However, do not be misled by this classification system. Remember that several standards can and should be addressed while reading all texts, particularly during a *first* close reading.

In case the bibliography is overwhelming as a starting point, use the list shown on pages 32–35, which captures my true favorites for intermediate grade students— picture books, poems, and short stories that I consider must-haves on my close reading list. Each is annotated so that you can make a decision about whether the source would be worth checking out for reading with *your* students. A challenge when identifying complex text for children in the later elementary grades is to make sure that "complex" doesn't mean that the content is conceptually beyond what is appropriate for preadolescents.

When TEXT SELECTION Goes OFF Track

Let's face it: Text selection can go awry. The following are some pitfalls to avoid when choosing books for close reading.

1. A hyperfocus on Lexile. There are *so many* features of a text that should get our attention beyond a formulaic estimate based on word frequency and sentence length. Remember to take into account other considerations as well.

2. The temptation to restrict students' reading to qualitative complexities that lie within your comfort zone or personal preferences. Many of us value, above all, complex meaning in a text, and we may select only literature and informational sources that reflect that bias. Remember that the Common Core is about equal opportunity complexity.

3. Dropping complex text into the curriculum in a hit-or-miss way. Choosing a text for close reading just because it is "hard" will make the reading an empty and frustrating experience rather than an opportunity for deep learning. Some of the texts mentioned above—for example, the poem "Abraham Lincoln" and the picture book *Mercedes and the Chocolate Pilot*—would be best situated after students have some initial understanding of the historic periods they represent. Other texts might benefit from thematic or topical foundations. Close reading will be much more successful with attention to what the Common Core calls "coherence." This means that the first text will anchor the next; the third text will build upon the first two—and so forth. This is the way units and text studies should be designed.

4. A lack of careful planning or preparation. Teachers will need a thorough understanding of the text themselves before they can guide students deeper into its meaning. Translation: We can't grab a book or find a poem two minutes before the lesson begins and expect that our instruction will go well. Careful planning will be more important than ever. In fact, begin with texts you know and love. You are already familiar with the complexities of these texts, making it easier to approach them for deep meaning.

Lesson Planning for Close Reading

When we think of a lesson "plan," we envision a road map of sorts that will lead us and our students through the twists and turns of some instructional task. Beginning here, and continuing in the next several chapters, we will create that formal "plan" for one lesson. The intent is that this process will be generative, that you will use it to develop your own close reading lessons.

First, I'd like us to consider the *text selection* and *preparation* that precedes the step-by-step lesson we will ultimately plan. In the remainder of this chapter, I discuss text selection in detail. In the following chapter, Chapter 3, I focus on additional points related to preparing for close reading. In the remainder of the book, I offer guidance for completing the planning for the lesson itself: before, during, and after close reading.

Applying What We Know

Choosing a Complex Text For Today's Lesson

Take a look at the template shown in Figure 2.3 (a blank version can also be found in Appendix I and at **www.corwin.com/closerreading**) called Preparing for Close Reading. The teachers with whom I work find it a valuable tool to lean on when planning lessons. I've filled it in based on the personal narrative, "She Was *THAT* Kind of Lady" (see Figure 2.2) so you can get the hang of the kind of considerations I make. It is not essential that you fill these boxes in every time you teach close reading. What you should do every time is at least *think* about the considerations listed on this form, because you always need to know *why* you are choosing a particular complex text for close reading and the challenges your students will face as they read it.

Step-by-step, throughout the next few chapters, we will develop a lesson for a hypothetical class of fourth graders using the text "She Was *THAT* Kind of Lady." This is a memoir, a personal story about my own grandmother. We cared for her in her home, an old New England homestead that had been in our family since the earliest years of the twentieth century. *What have we done?* I wondered to myself on move-in day, looking around the dilapidated old Victorian. This would test the mettle of my husband's skills as a home renovator for decades to come (or so it seemed). And my ten-year-old daughter? How would she handle the change in lifestyle that now included a very aged great-grandma with limited mobility and a short-term memory that wasn't working so well either?

Turns out this was one of the best decisions of our lives. We're still there, minus Gram who departed this earth now over a decade ago. But the walls continue to echo her story set down for students here. Students won't need all this background, but I share it here to encourage you to select texts for your students that you "connect" with too, as it helps you model engagement with the text. Our students are constantly reading us as we are teaching—if you really admire a text, chances are you will get them to admire it too.

The second part of the blank template, Planning for Close Reading (see Appendix I), will be addressed in the next chapter, when I describe preparing for close reading instruction.

Following on page 42 is a more detailed rationale for my text selection, so you can be privy to the thinking behind my brief notes on the template.

Figure 2.2

She Was *THAT* Kind of Lady

By Nancy Boyles

1.

She wasn't a modern kind of grandma. She didn't have blonde hair or pierced ears. And I don't think she ever owned a pair of sneakers or even a pair of shorts. Her gray hair was long, but it disappeared behind a lot of hairpins at the back of her head. She mostly wore "house dresses," plaid or flowered cotton creations that sometimes buttoned or snapped down the front and sometimes tied with a sash. My grandma was not what you'd call a "fashionable lady."

2.

Mostly she wasn't "Grandma" either. She wasn't Nana or Nonnie or Grandmother. Most of the time, she was just plain Gram.

Gram was the kind of lady who did plain "Gram things." Like the wash. When I was really young, Gram would do the wash every day in an old-fashioned wringer washing machine. She'd feed one of those house dresses through a couple of cylinders, and it would come out on the other side, flat as a pancake, all the water wrung out of it. I couldn't decide which was scarier, that machine that looked like it could just as easily grab and flatten Gram's hand if it got too close or the dark, damp cellar where the machine lived.

Then Gram would haul a whole basket of flat, wet dresses and aprons and towels out to the clothesline that stretched from the back door almost to the garage. She'd hang those clothes up and let them soak in the fresh-air smell all day long until they were good and dry (and stiff as a board!). Gram kept using that clothesline for years, even after Pop bought her a fancy new clothes dryer for the basement. She was *that* kind of lady.

3.

Gram was the kind of lady who would stand next to Pop behind the counter in Baldwin's Store, even before most women had "real" jobs. "Forty-three years in the grocery business," she'd say later on. "I went in one day to give Pop a hand . . ." But what she said back then was, "Help yourself to a Popsicle." I'd reach my arm down deep in the big chest freezer and try to decide: Which frosty treat would it be this week? Even then I'd almost always choose chocolate.

4.

Gram was the kind of lady whose other "real" job was in the kitchen in her old gray Victorian on South Main Street. And, oh, that kitchen always smelled so good. It smelled like Gram's kitchen: succotash in summer and a huge glass bowl of cut-up peaches. Jars and jars of homemade bread and butter pickles and chili sauce in the fall. Roast beef on Christmas. And fried chicken all year long. "I made two pies on Wednesday and two pies on Saturday. Pop was an old pie face," she'd say. Sometimes the pie was lemon meringue. Gram knew that was my favorite.

5.

Gram was the kind of lady who looked like a queen sitting alongside Pop on the front seat of their big, white Cadillac with the longest fins in the history of the world. They sure *seemed* like the longest fins when that car first pulled into the driveway in front of the little house where I grew up. "Where'd you get those fins, Gram?" my brother asked. This wasn't a brand-new car, but it looked like an important car. And Gram looked important, too, perched in the passenger seat guiding Pop around town:

"Turn here, Chollie." (In New England, "Charlie" seemed to lose his "r".)

(Continued)

"Remember, there's a stop sign at the next corner." Gram never learned to drive, but Pop couldn't have driven anywhere without her. In fact, Pop wanted Gram by his side every minute of every day. Gram, however, didn't mind a little time to herself.

6.

Gram was the kind of lady who could spend hours just rocking in the old wicker rocker on the front porch. I used to think that every problem in the whole universe passed through that porch at one time or another. People would walk past, out for an evening stroll, and someone would holler up, "How ya doin', Vernie?"

"That's Mabel Worthington," Gram would whisper to me. Before you knew it, Mabel was coming up the walk and the screen door was creaking closed behind her.

"Hottest summer we've ever had, wouldn't you say, Mabel?" Gram began with small talk, but soon the talk would turn to more pressing matters like who was in the hospital or the next town election. And the night would end with an ice cream soda, Gram's famous root beer float, of course.

7.

Gram was the kind of lady who collected people. Maybe it was because of all those years waiting on customers that she knew so many folks. Or maybe it was her rice pudding. Anytime someone was sick, Gram was on the doorstep with a bowl of rice pudding—and a smile. Many of those friends were still returning that goodwill decades later.

8.

The steeple clock on the Congregational church across the street from Gram's house marked the passing of hours . . . and seasons . . . and years . . . and decades. And still Gram rocked in the old wicker chair on the front porch. But now, the little girl sitting next to her was not me, but *my* little girl.

"Tell that story again, Gramma Vernie, you know the one about the . . ." my daughter would beg. And her great grandma would begin one more time—

There was the story of the escaped slave who lived right next door on Church Street.

There were the stories of digging clams with her father in Stony Creek (seventy-five cents a quart) and packing bread at Prann's bakery (the 6 a.m. shift).

There were Pop stories: "Pop always said I had the best legs in Branford." "Pop loved to play cards, but he'd get so mad when I'd beat him."

There was the near-drowning story: "Those fresh boys threw me into the Branford River; they knew I couldn't swim."

And there were school stories: The ones about school usually ended with how she'd always wanted to be a teacher, but her parents didn't have the money to send her to college.

"Well," she shrugged, "that's just the way things were in those days."

9.

"You would have been a great teacher," I always replied, loudly enough for Gram's aging ears. By now, Gram's legs weren't working so well either, and sometimes she could tell a whole story in the time it took her to hobble with her walker from her rocker on the porch to her chair in her kitchen, our kitchen.

They both needed a bit of care—the old gray Victorian and "the old gray mare" (as Gram so often called herself). And so we moved in to help with both. In her most golden years, Gram was the kind of lady who never complained. If there were aches and pains in those ninety-eight-year-old bones, she never said. Instead, she sat in the sunniest corner of the kitchen crocheting lap robes for "old people" and sipped tea with milk. "That's the way the English like their tea," she'd remind me. Then she'd smile one of her magical Gram smiles. She was *that* kind of lady.

Figure 2.3

Preparing For Close Reading

(Sample Template)

Title of text: "She Was *THAT* Kind of Lady"

Curriculum Connection

Reasons for selecting this text: Good example of a personal narrative; shows depth of character as a text of this sort should; shows the impact of the setting on the person; reasonably complex for fourth graders

Theme connection/inquiry question: What qualities do you admire most in a role model or everyday hero?

Placement of this text within a lesson sequence: This text would work well as an initial lesson because it addresses a topic to which students can relate while exploring a new theme/inquiry.

Complexity of the Text

Lexile (if available) or other readability measure: 1070; Flesch Kincaid: 5.2

Qualitative complexities of this text:

- Knowledge demands: No connection to small town New England life in the early part of the twentieth century
- Meaning: Gram is a complex character to understand—her own values and her impact on others
- Language: Lots of unfamiliar vocabulary: succotash, (Cadillac) fins, house dresses, wringer washing machine
- Structure: Text is nonlinear; not a problem/solution structure

Challenges for students reading this text:

N/A without knowledge of the particular class

Learning Points From the First Close Reading

Approaching the Text

_____ Teacher reads entire text aloud first, then goes back and reads chunk by chunk

_____ Students read entire text first for a general impression; then the teacher reads chunk by chunk

_____ Teacher reads by chunk without an initial read-through by either the teacher or the students

_____ I have determined appropriate text chunks: places to pause and ask questions.

Considerations for Close Reading, Part I

● Curriculum Connection

Reasons for selecting this text: I consider this memoir a valuable close reading text for intermediate-grade students because it is a good example of this genre, providing lots of insight into the values that motivate the central character (person). It also demonstrates the impact of the time and place on the individual, another critical element of memoir, and is reasonably complex for the grade level for which it will be used. Interestingly, the Common Core classifies memoir and personal narrative as "informational" despite their literary structure. This certainly broadens our definition of this category.

Theme connection/inquiry question: There is clearly an important theme or inquiry question within this text that readers can explore: What qualities do we most admire in a role model or everyday hero? Always make sure your close reading text has a worthy theme; it's an important aspect of complexity. And remember a worthy theme offers a gateway for students to the close reading of other memoirs or personal narratives that have similar or contrasting themes, thereby increasing students' knowledge about both the theme and the genre. (While there are technical differences between personal narrative and memoir, I do not think this distinction is critical to students of this age.)

Placement of this text within a lesson sequence: This text could be a good *first* foray into this inquiry question (or theme) related to "everyday heroes" through personal accounts because many children look up to their grandparents. Now we will ask *why* a grandparent (or anyone) commands our respect. But as you select your text, always consider what *other* texts would work well within a thematic or inquiry unit based on that text. Also, consider where each would fall in a sequence of the texts you select. In this case, perhaps "She Was *THAT* Kind of Lady" could be followed by these texts:

- "My Granddaddy Is My Daddy Too," a poem from *In Daddy's Arms I Am Tall: African Americans Celebrating Fathers* by Javaka Steptoe. This poem describes the extra special things about one grandpa serving the Daddy role: "can carve whistles out of wood . . . catch fifteen fish in a day . . . has feet nearly two feet long."

- I might then go to *Luba, the Angel of Bergen-Belsen* (Luba Tryszynska-Frederick, Ann Marshall, and Michelle McCann). This picture book tells the true story of a young World War II nurse in Germany who finds fifty-four orphaned children abandoned behind a concentration camp. Despite the danger to her own life, she figures out a way to feed and comfort them amid a harsh winter of disease, starvation, and war: "But they are someone's children and they are hungry."

- I'd like to end this inquiry with a text about an everyday hero who was a child close to the age of the children in my hypothetical fourth-grade class. One possibility is *The Boy Who Spoke Up*, a short video clip accessed at http://www.katu.com/news/local/Everyday-Heroes-The-boy-who-spoke-up-truman-templeton-209762721.html. In less than three minutes, seventeen-year-old Truman Templeton explains how he found the courage to speak up about his classmate's plot to bring bombs to his high school.

● Complexity of the Text

Lexile or other readability measure: It's relatively easy to get a Lexile for any book at approximately the third-grade level or higher (http://www.scholastic.com/bookwizard) but more of a challenge to get this measurement for a portion of a text. Furthermore, Lexile is not recommended as a measure of text difficulty for poetry (or for any text below about a mid-second-grade level). Lexile Analyzer (http://www.lexile.com/analyzer) is somewhat helpful in this regard, but it doesn't support Word documents; everything must first be converted to plain text, and then the passage can't surpass a specified word limit. The Lexile for a few paragraphs from "She Was *THAT* Kind of Lady" was reported to be 1070, technically a bit high for fourth grade. The Flesch Kincaid readability score available through Microsoft Spell Check revealed a grade-level equivalent of 5.2. Lack of reliability between readability measures is one of the reasons that the Lexile number should be used cautiously. Either way, this text is near enough to the identified range to be acceptable for fourth graders who will have careful, close reading guidance from their teacher. For even better validation, I can report that I've used this text with students in Grades 4 and 5. It works.

Qualitative complexities of this text: The qualitative complexities of this text initially have to do with students' lack of connection to life in a small New England town during the first half of the twentieth century (actually *any* part of the twentieth century . . . yikes!). Some of the vocabulary used in relation to this time and place will also make the text harder to understand: succotash, (Cadillac) fins, wringer washing machine, house dresses, the reference to the song "The Old Gray Mare," and so on. There is much to infer about Gram—not just her values and motivations but her impact on the other people in her life as well—adding to the complexity of the meaning. Even more subtle and potentially challenging are the inferences a reader needs to make about the the narrator: Her feelings for her grandmother can be inferred but are not explicitly stated. The text's nonlinear structure, offering a kind of "Gram mosaic" will challenge readers who look solely for a sequence of events that begins with a problem and ends with a solution; this is *not* a problem/solution story.

We will think about other aspects of our preparation for close reading in the following chapter. Before moving to that, though, pause and reflect—with your professional learning community, a colleague, or on your own—on what you've here learned about text complexity. The following questions will get you started.

Reflecting on What We Know

1. In what ways do you now have a better understanding of text complexity and its relationship to close reading than you did before reading this chapter? Did anything in this chapter surprise you?

2. Which qualitative features of text complexity do you think will be most challenging for your students? Why?

3. Which of my favorite picture books, poems, or short stories might work well with your students? Why do you think so?

4. Think about some of the texts you love to read with your students. Based on various features of complexity and my criteria for selecting texts (or your own criteria), which of your personal favorites appear to be a good fit for close reading?

5. Choose a book or other text you have not used before that would be appropriate for a close reading lesson. Analyze it according to the criteria on the chart in Figure 2.1, Is This Text Complex? on page 28. (This is the text you will use to develop each part of your close reading plan as we move through the rest of this book, so choose carefully!) Share your selection—and rationale—with your colleagues.

6. Using the blank Preparing for Close Reading template (see Appendix I or go to **www.corwin.com/closerreading**), fill in only the boxes for Curriculum Connection and Complexity of the Text for the complex text you've selected. What was hard about doing this? What was easy? What questions do you have? If possible, share and discuss your work here with one or more colleagues also working on close reading.

CHAPTER 3

Getting in the Mindset of Close Reading

Instructional Shift

Before the Common Core	With the Common Core
Lesson focus: The lesson was often driven by a specific *objective*: Teachers taught to one, often isolated objective, such as identifying character traits, finding the theme, and so on.	**Lesson focus:** For an initial close reading, the lesson is driven by the *text*. The first reading is intended to be more *general*: How much meaning can you make the *first* time you read a text?

The Instructional Shift

Once you've identified a good, complex text, the next step is to decide how you want to use this text for close reading. With the Common Core State Standards, we are asked to rethink the purpose of our instruction to focus more on the *text* and less on a specific *objective*—at least the first time we read a text with our students. This is an important shift with significant implications for our instruction. Later, when we return to the text to reread it, there will be opportunity for more attention to specific skills and strategies, as explained in Chapter 8 of this book. But our first reading should focus on gathering as much meaning as possible, examining both the content and the craft. This point leads us to the following question: *What specifically do we want our initial close reading of a text to look like and accomplish?*

Focusing broadly on meaning during reading hardly sounds like breaking news, and indeed it has always been the overarching intent of many classroom teachers as well as many top educators and authors who write about the teaching of reading. But unfortunately high-stakes assessments that measure a repertoire of discrete comprehension skills have led publishers of basals and other programs—and thus, in turn, teachers—in a different direction that boiled everything down to an alignment between specific skills taught and specific skills tested.

We want our first close reading to explore the richness of the text as a whole as opposed to looking at one aspect of the text. In the recent past, our reading has focused on individual components of a text separately. We studied characters one day and the problem on another day. We might then move on to setting or theme or author's purpose. Whether we used programs that parsed the elements this way or worked with a curriculum we created, we reasoned that breaking the reading process into discrete components led to good skill development. It is much like the analogy of "not seeing the forest for the trees." In the reality of how skill-based instruction played out in classrooms, students rarely got to appreciate the beauty of the whole "forest," how all parts of a text worked together to generate meaning. Great works of literature and important informational pieces were reduced to conduits (lone "trees") for learning *about* reading.

The practice of close reading asks us to rethink students' reading process to maximize their understanding of the content itself. Let them read a text the first time not to get better at a skill (which yields only limited gratification for children), but so they might close the book after the final chapter and declare, "Wow, I *loved* that story" or "What an amazing article!" A good story (or informational piece) is like a collage, a whole host of carefully and creatively arranged elements that are more meaningful when viewed together than when dissected one fragment at a time.

This does not mean that on a first reading we want students to simply graze the surface of a text for enjoyment of the plot or recognition of the main idea. On the contrary, we want them to begin to understand the interaction of all of a text's critical features. Among the features we want intermediate-grade students to explore in the first round of close reading of fiction or informational texts are the following:

- The narrator or author
- Characters or people
- Problem or issue

- Setting or context

- Solution or outcome

There should also be some awareness of these facets of a text:

- The author's word choice and the way it contributes to meaning

- The way the structure of the text supports the content

- A sense of the role of illustrations or graphics

- Places to apply metacognitive strategies such as visualizing and wondering

Tracking all these elements simultaneously is the way "real" readers make meaning. Will students finish their first reading with an in-depth understanding of all of these? No, but if we teach them how to read closely, they will be off to a solid start. When they return to the text for the second reading, or the one after that, they will have the opportunity to refine their understanding.

Scheduling an Initial Close Reading Lesson

20 to 30 Minutes Once a Week

Close reading should fit purposefully into the day in the part of our literacy block that we may call *shared reading*—where the whole class works together for a few minutes grappling with a text. In your school you may simply call this a whole-class lesson.

Shared reading is often associated with primary-grade instruction, when the teacher uses a "big book" or other text to which the entire class can have easy visual access. Students gather around the teacher, and they would enjoy the text together in a manner that approximates "lap reading" at home. Fortunately, shared reading has now also found a niche in upper-grade classrooms; its format—whole-class instruction, where the focus is on interaction and a sense of community—is terrific for the intermediate grades.

An initial close reading lesson will take twenty to about thirty minutes. Many intermediate-grade students can't focus on much of anything for more than about half an hour. Also, close reading lessons that go on and on will steal minutes from other components of the literacy block that are also important. When you return to the text with your students to reread it, focusing on a particular skill or strategy, your lesson may be more "mini." When you reread, you are addressing one specific aspect of it, such as locating places in a news article where the author's word choice has an impact on the tone of the piece or noting how a mystery has been crafted to inspire you to predict in certain places. This often needs less time than you will need for deconstructing a whole text initially.

I generally select one complex, close reading "anchor text" per week. I prefer the term *anchor text* over *mentor text* because this text "anchors" related follow-up lessons later in the week (and mentor text is a term most associated with using literature to provide students with role models—mentors—for writing.)

Allowing the *Text Itself* to Be Our Objective

Beyond the logistics of scheduling close reading, there is also the question of *how* we approach close reading instruction. We have been so programmed over the last several years to deliver sharply focused lessons that address one—and only one— objective, that reimagining instruction as driven by the text itself and not by some small component of the reading process is difficult to grasp.

"You mean we should now have two or three objectives for close reading?" teachers ask, trying to wrap their heads around this new idea.

That's not what I mean. I mean we should help children read the way *we* read. We don't sit down with a new book and say to ourselves, "Now let's see, today I think I'll try to identify the problem in the story. Maybe I'll also look for similes, and I'll try to locate where the main character changes, too."

No, we open that book with the intent of understanding and enjoying everything about it, losing ourselves in the magic. Its content, language, and structure all work together to make meaning in our mind.

"This is what we want for our kids, too," I explain. "We'll get as much meaning out of the text during our first close reading as we can. It's more about reading for a purpose than reading to meet an *objective*."

In fact, our lesson plan for an initial close reading of a text should say something like this:

> *The student will read [this complex text] closely for deep understanding.*

Or if your district requires "I" statements framed from the learner's point of view, it might say this:

> *I will read [this complex text] closely for deep understanding.*

"What did you say?" teachers want to know, eyebrows furrowed, sure that they didn't hear me correctly the first time I explain this. Although teachers tell me that *they* like this idea of a close reading *purpose* and see its merit as a path to more natural teaching and authentic learning, they're quite sure that their administrators will hold a different view:

"We're *required* to have a *specific* objective; we even have to post it," they insist.

Some also add that without a specific objective they will get "marked down" during lesson observations. "Just" reading "closely for deep understanding" won't cut it. Clearly, we will need to get administrators on board with this "new normal" for lesson intent as well. I expect both teachers and administrators will need to explore this shift for a while before its value sinks in. They will need to see that for close reading, the intent is to make meaning first through observing and then by analyzing. There is still a need for skill building and explicit instruction, but that will come later.

The Work of a First Close Reading: Making Meaning

For a first close reading, the goal is for students to build a broad understanding of a text, keeping track of the way the content, language, and structure interact to make meaning. Although most of this will be determined through observation, the roots of analysis will take hold here, too.

Students need to begin by seeing—really seeing—what's there on each page. While this seems obvious, barely worthy of mention, I must point out that this is not the way many children read. They may miss the fine points. They may even miss the most basic information.

Because much of the meaning in an elementary-level text seems pretty obvious to us, we assume it must be equally clear to those nine-year-olds sitting in front of us; we immediately jump into challenging questions and then wonder why lots of students are lost. Whenever I take the time to check in on something that I'm *sure* will be a too-easy question, I find that at least a couple of students are confused. I also discover that many of those sweet nine-year-olds missed the meaning in the first go-round because, honestly, they were not listening or reading themselves with any level of personal accountability.

Turn your brains to the "on" position, I want to say. What I actually say is, "I'll read this page again (or you read it again), and you listen/look for what the author is telling us." One of the challenges we face with close reading is getting students to pay attention to an author's words the *first* time, to develop a sense of accountability to the text.

Realistically, even with careful observation, students won't appreciate everything about a text in their first reading. When text is complex, we'll want to come back to it for subsequent lessons to dig deeper. But even in an initial close reading, students' thinking will quite naturally segue from simply observing the words on the page to beginning to analyze what those words mean. For example, we may ask students to identify how an author grabbed our attention at the beginning of a story. That's a good first question to ask sixth graders for Langston Hughes's short story "Thank You, M'am." They are immediately intrigued that the old woman, rather than falling victim to the teenage boy who tries to steal her purse, instead pursues her assailant and takes charge of the situation. "What will this woman do next?" students wonder. They are hooked.

But let's not stop there when we can push just a little harder and move from basic *noticing* to *analyzing:* "Why was this action surprising?" And finally, "What do you think the author wants us to see through this woman's behavior?"

Students tell me: "I was surprised because I thought the lady was going to scream." "She's spunky." "She's strong." "She's willing to stand up for what's right." They don't have the theme yet. However, they can now make some informed predictions about this character's future actions.

Then in a subsequent lesson, we can move on to deeper analysis. We might focus on a character study of the boy, Roger, or the old woman, Mrs. Louella Bates

For a first close reading, the goal is for students to build a broad understanding of a text, keeping track of the way the content, language, and structure interact to make meaning.

Washington Jones. This would take us even deeper into the text—the thoughts, words, actions, and interactions of each of these characters. There is a place for both observing and analyzing in a close reading lesson, though in a first read-through there will be more observing and less analyzing—and the reverse will be true when revisiting a text.

For us, the process is so automatic that we don't even realize that we're "looking for" anything. For our students, though, it's different. They are just learning what good readers do, and it is our job to move their thinking along by pointing out to them what the author expects them to notice, what will best support their understanding of the meaning in the text. Some of these points are exclusive to literature or information; some apply to all text.

Planning an Initial Close Reading Lesson

The Attributes of Text That Help Readers Make Meaning

If our close reading mission is to shift our instructional priorities to gathering as much meaning as possible from a text, we need to consider more thoroughly what students should look for as they read in order to achieve that goal.

Who Is Telling This Story—or Providing This Information?

One of the first discoveries a reader should make in a literary text is this: Who is the narrator? Is it someone "inside" or "outside" the story? With a first-person narrator, you realize immediately whose side of the story you're getting. In the past, I think we've regularly asked this "narrator" question but haven't then pushed students' thinking beyond this simple recognition to ask why it makes a difference:

- What does this person care about?

- What worries or motivates him or her?

- How would this story/article be different if [another character/person] was telling or explaining it?

Once we've observed the important evidence—in this case, information regarding who the narrator *is*—we can *build* on it for analysis.

Literary text with a first-person narrator serves us well because of the way it illuminates point of view, a good reason for teaching with lots of first-person texts. But we will also teach with plenty of texts with a third-person narrator, one who is "outside" the story. Recognizing perspective in these texts is equally important, though more challenging. We can make this a little easier for students by explaining that often the author speaks through the voice of the main character, the protagonist. The antagonist (bad guy/girl) may reflect values opposite to the author's views.

I frequently use the book *Weslandia* by Paul Fleischman to make this point. The narrator makes comments like, "He'd refused to shave half his head, the hairstyle worn by all the other boys, despite his father's bribe of five dollars." And this one: "Passing his neighborhood's two styles of housing—garage on the left and garage on the right—Wesley alone dreamed of more exciting forms of shelter."

Whose side does the narrator support here? Is the author poking fun at Wesley or at Wesley's father? What do you think the author wants you to recognize about succumbing to peer pressure and asserting one's individuality?

With informational text, point of view is more challenging still and, for Common Core purposes, perhaps even more critical to students' comprehension. The issue is this: There is no such thing as an "objective" text; everything is written (or told) from *someone's* point of view. But young children don't see this. They see the words on the page of their social studies textbook or in a news article and regard them as "facts." They trust that the author who put them there is knowledgeable, researched her subject thoroughly, and presented the information in a fair-minded way. As teachers, we know we can't be quite so trusting.

One of our important jobs when we use informational text is to teach students to be critical consumers of what they read. Point of view becomes evident through the author's purpose:

- What was this author's purpose in providing this information?
- What does she or he want us to know and believe?
- Is the author trying to convince us of something?

Then, for deeper analysis, we can examine whether there might be anyone else with a different perspective on the situation.

What Do We Know About Story Parts and Informational Details?

We can begin our work with text elements with questions about characters or important people:

- Who are they?
- What are their names?

Basic, yes, but how often do students talk about these essential text elements with language no more specific than *he* or *she*? These observations are equally important for both literary and informational sources. We can then look more closely:

- Who is the most important person here—or the main character?
- Do these people (or characters) stay the same throughout the text, or do they change?

Figure 3.1

Reading to Make Meaning in Literary and Informational Texts

Narrator

- Literary: Is the narrator a character in the story? If so, who is it?
- Literary: Is the narrator someone "outside" the story (the author)?
- Informational: What is the author's purpose? What does she or he want me to know and believe?
- What does the narrator/author seem to care about? How do I know?

Characters/People

- Who are the characters/people?
- Who is the most important character (person)—and how can I tell?
- Do the characters/people stay the same throughout the text, or do they change? How do they change?
- What personal traits do I notice, and how do they make a difference?
- Do the characters/people have different points of view or the same point of view?

Setting/Context

- *When* does the story or situation take place: past, present, future?
- Does the time and place seem to be important to the events? How?
- Does the setting stay the same throughout the story or situation, or does it change? Where?
- Does the author give a lot of details about the setting before telling about the problem?

Problem/Events

- *Is* there a problem? If so, what is the *main* problem?
- What happens before the problem gets solved?
- Can I name several important details? Why are they important?

Solution/Outcome/Ending

- How does the story or situation end?
- If there's a problem, does it get solved? How?
- Does the author "wrap up" the story or situation, or does she or he leave unanswered questions?
- Is the ending happy or sad?

Illustrations/Graphics/Text Features

- How do the illustrations/graphics add to my understanding of the story or information?
- Are there chapter titles, bolded words, subheadings, or other text features that support my understanding? What are they? How do they help me?

Words

- What important words from this text will I need in order to talk about it?

Craft

- Are there standout features of the language and structure that add to meaning?

Metacognitive Strategies

- Where does the author want me to do the following: picture, wonder, predict, notice important clues, figure out, connect?

- If they change, where does the change occur?

- Is there evidence of a standout personal trait that makes a difference to the way the character/person acts?

- How does it make a difference?

Much of a first close reading will be spent identifying who the text is about and answering questions related to other basic text elements. For literary text this means story parts: setting, problem, actions, outcome, and how the story ends. For informational text, students will be looking to clarify the topic and the most important supporting facts and details. Rather than describe each element in detail here, it would be more efficient as you prepare for close reading to review Figure 3.1, Reading to Make Meaning in Literary and Informational Texts.

What Else Should Readers Look For in Their First Close Reading of a Text?

Beyond basic text elements, there are other aspects of a text that will help to form a foundation of understanding. As you study the text you will use for a lesson, think about and perhaps even flag the text with sticky notes with questions and prompts that help students attend to the text in these ways:

- Are there **illustrations or graphics** to note? In a first close reading, students may not be able to learn *everything* about an illustration, photograph, chart, or the like that could inform their comprehension. Some of these may need more serious investigation during a reread. But the first journey through the text should at least alert readers that these supports are present, sparking some first impressions.

- What about **important words**? Which ones will be the most useful in talking about the text afterward? For informational text, these will probably be key content words. For literary text, characters' names, places, and words connected to the problem and solution will be important. This concept of important words is an area we often overlook—and we shouldn't. How can students even summarize a text if they haven't recognized the key words? I'm not suggesting anything deep here. For instance, in the book *The Raft* students should recognize that *raft* is a key word. In an article about the Wright brothers, they'd probably want the word *airplane*. Important words often recur several times.

- What about the **crafting** of the text? Are there standout features of the language and structure that jump right out at you? Some examples might be similes, repeated lines and phrases, flashbacks, or unique ways to place and shape print. An author's craft can often be analyzed more thoroughly during a subsequent close reading. But some crafts are evident right away.

- And finally, is the **theme or main idea** within reach during the initial reading, or will that demand a return to the text for closer examination? While it's true that theme and main idea aren't typically right there on the page in the same way that other meaning is spelled out (literally), there will be many occasions when careful reading will reveal the message to students even before the last page. We can encourage this by *always* talking about a text's theme or main idea. Then students will know to think about it. Sometimes of course, there are multiple themes or very complex themes. For those, we will need to come back on another day for a deeper look.

What Metacognitive Strategies Might Readers Need Now or in Subsequent Lessons With This Text?

You've probably noticed that there is no mention of metacognitive strategies in the Common Core—attention to processes such as visualizing, synthesizing, questioning, and inferring that help students "think about their thinking." This lack of attention to metacognition is making lots of educators nervous because we know that taught well, strategies can enhance students' comprehension in important ways.

Why this blatant omission? I suspect that the reason we don't find strategies referenced in the standards is that the Common Core is about the endgame: What can students understand about a text when they have *finished* reading it? Metacognitive strategies are about the journey to that destination—the processes involved. With or without explicit mention in the Standards document, we can—and should—encourage students to use metacognitive strategies to construct meaning. We just need to make sure that for close reading, strategy use leads to deeper understanding of the text.

In the past, some educators focused too much on having students learn and apply individual strategies. If the strategy du jour was *visualizing*, all students did was report the images they created in their mind. Exactly how these mental pictures improved comprehension was never completely clear. In fact, applying strategies was largely random, more about *having* a strategy than *being* strategic: *I have a connection. . . . I have a question. . . . I have an inference.*

We can do better.

We can put strategies to work as a real tool for helping students access meaning—the author's meaning. An author crafts a text in intentional ways that encourage readers to use particular strategies in particular places. For example, when the author describes a scene in great detail, what does the author want you to do? That's a good place to make a picture in your mind. When the author leaves you hanging at the end of a page or at the end of a chapter, now what does the author want you to do? Perhaps you should make a prediction. Being strategic in this way leads readers deeper into text—the entire point of close reading and an important goal of the Common Core.

By activating metacognitive strategies and looking carefully for the kinds of evidence noted above, readers will finish their first close reading of a text with a sound foundation of textual knowledge. But we also need to be aware of what that first reading probably *can't* accomplish. Those fine points will bring us back to the text for a second or third round—this time with a more pointed focus for more thorough work with specific literacy skills and strategies. Maybe we want students to make a connection to another text. Maybe we want them to consider alternate perspectives: How would the story (or events of a situation) be different if told from another character's or stakeholder's point of view? Maybe we will reread to investigate figurative language more thoroughly. Chapter 8 elaborates on this follow-up instruction.

How Might We Chunk and Approach the Text?

There is one final issue with which teachers must come to terms before the lesson can begin: How will the text be read and in what size chunks? This is a bigger deal than you might think as it will directly contribute to students' enjoyment of close reading and whether or not they are successful with it. You have several choices for approaching the text:

Option 1: *The teacher reads the entire text aloud first, no close reading involved, just to provide a sense of the story or information or the sound of the language.* This works well if the text is a poem where the cadence of language will be lost when you begin pulling the lines apart word by word. It is impractical if the text is too long, and it is actually detrimental if you have a story with a much-anticipated solution at the end of it. Lots of students mentally check out once they know "what happens in the end." In this case, they are unlikely to invest much mental energy in the close reading that follows where you are asking them to take the text apart syllable by syllable; they've already gotten what they came for.

poetry

Option 2: *Ask students to read the whole text first themselves before embarking on the close reading of it.* I like this when I want a general sense of what students can figure out on their own from a text that is challenging—but not so challenging that the first impression will be "There's no way I will ever understand this." If the text appears too hard, some students never get past that sense of defeat.

short article

Option 3: *Read the text chunk by chunk right away, no initial exposure.* I use this method a lot. It's the way I typically approach picture books where *I* do the reading or short stories or articles where I sometimes have students read alone or in partnerships. Picture books are usually too long for a "quick" read-through, and they often tell stories with a problem and solution. Reading closely chunk by chunk keeps kids on board with the story as it unfolds.

most read-alouds

For optimal understanding, you need to get the size of the text chunk right, too. With a picture book, it's easy: a single page or a two-page spread. Of course, you can focus on individual sentences, phrases, or even words on a page. Poems are easily divided into stanzas. Short stories and articles are trickier because you need to figure out logical stopping points with chunks that are meaningful, but not so long that students will lose their way. When in doubt, shorter is better.

When OUR CLOSE READING AGENDA Goes OFF Track

Low expectations for students. As noted early in this chapter, the work of close reading is all about observing and analyzing a text in order to make meaning, whether you subscribe to the instructional model described in this book or another model. With complex texts, there will be lots of meaning to track; it goes with the territory. Lots of little things can go wrong in pursuit of this, but right now I'm especially concerned about one big thing. A serious "off-track outcome" I've witnessed related to preparing for close reading is that a few teachers are too quick to throw up their hands and declare, "My kids can't do this." I came face-to-face with such a situation in a workshop I presented recently. I had given a group of fourth-grade teachers a short informational piece about Amelia Earhart. When I noticed several minutes later that one member of this group had nothing written on her Preparing for Close Reading template, I asked if I could help. "This is too hard," she told me unequivocally. "They'll never be able to do this."

Some teachers are worried that they will not recognize everything important about a text so that they can, in turn, help their students see it, too.

We just looked at each other for a few seconds, this teacher and I. I was not about to back down. I had used this article successfully numerous times with populations of fourth graders much needier than the students in this school. "Let's look at this together," I suggested. We then went through the first paragraph phrase by phrase. All the kinds of evidence we'd just discussed were right there on the page, an almost perfect example of a well-constructed informational text. When this teacher and I looked closely at this text together, she could see that her students really *could* handle it. And perhaps just as important, *she* could handle it as well.

Teacher insecurities: I *hope* I'm doing this right. A second, related issue surrounding preparation for close reading is that some teachers are worried that they will not recognize everything important about a text so that they can, in turn, help their students see it, too. They hesitate to get started with close reading for fear that they're not "doing it right." This is particularly true regarding their understanding of the way a text has been *crafted*. We feel pretty well prepared in recognizing meaning cues (hints at the theme, identification of character traits, and such). But when it comes to sorting out elements of craft and structure (an important focus of the Common Core), we sense that we're on shakier ground.

We should all try to cut ourselves some slack here. Nearly every time I read a book I find something new to talk about that I never saw in the text before, and very often this does have to do with the way the author has crafted it: word choice, repeated lines and phrases, transitions between stanzas, the list goes on. Over time, through our many encounters with complex text, we will gain a better sense of what to look for in the area of craft and structure. This is why using well-crafted text is so important. Many of the authors and works I cite in Chapter 2 will help you get started.

So my fear is this: Teachers with low expectations of what their students can achieve and lack of faith in themselves as good teachers of close reading will never give close reading a chance. To succeed with close reading, you need to be a believer. You need to believe in the power of complex text. You need to believe in the potential of close reading to unlock deep meaning. You need to believe in yourself. And most of all, you need to believe in your students—that they can do it. You also need to believe that close reading is worth the time and energy it will take to prepare for it properly—to set your close reading agenda with the rigor it deserves.

Learning Points For Today's Lesson

We have now identified the full range of instructional elements teachers need to consider before embarking on a close reading lesson and have even examined some teacher thinking that will impede a high-quality close reading agenda. We are now ready to apply what we have learned in this chapter to our hypothetical fourth-grade lesson by completing the remainder of the template Preparing for Close Reading. Remember that in Chapter 2 we filled in the first two cells and noted that in your own teaching you may be just *thinking* about these points rather than writing them down every time. Now, also complete the sections Learning Points From the First Close Reading and Approaching the Text (see Figure 3.2; for a blank version, see Appendix I and the book's companion website at **www.corwin.com/closereading**).

Following is a more detailed explanation of my thinking, which elaborates on the brief template notations.

Learning Points From the First Close Reading

A memoir is typically a study of the interaction of a person with a place, incorporating a collage of experiences. "She Was *THAT* Kind of Lady" fits this description well. Hence, learning points related to character and setting would be important to a first close reading. Students should come away with a reasonably accurate mental image of Gram's world. They should be able to describe Gram with several details. They should be able to explain how Gram interacted with the people around her and how these interactions made a difference. Most fourth graders, after a first careful reading, should also be able to explain the title—"She Was *THAT* Kind of Lady"—and from that tease out the theme.

Approaching the Text

For this text, any of the three options listed above for approaching it would be fine, so here, it really is a matter of personal preference. I decided not to have the students read the entire selection first or to read it to them myself because it is long and because the time it would take would not serve any clear purpose. This isn't a text where first impressions count for much. This is a story where Gram is revealed bit by bit, and I want students to savor each new detail as it comes their way.

There's something else to consider in approaching this text, too. This is a fairly long "short text." It can easily be broken into parts and read over two days. For close reading with complex text, you don't want to rush just to "cover" the material; there's too much to digest.

Figure 3.2

Preparing for Close Reading

Title of text: "She Was THAT Kind of Lady"

Curriculum Connection

Reasons for selecting this text: Good example of a personal narrative; shows depth of character as a text of this sort should; shows the impact of the setting on the person; reasonably complex for fourth graders

Theme connection/inquiry question: What qualities do you admire most in a role model or everyday hero?

Placement of this text within a lesson sequence: This text would work well as an initial lesson because it addresses a topic to which students can relate while exploring a new theme/inquiry.

Complexity of the Text

Lexile (if available) or other readability measure: 1070; Flesch Kincaid: 5.2

Qualitative complexities of this text:

- Knowledge demands: No connection to small town New England life in the early part of the twentieth century
- Meaning: Gram is a complex character to understand—her own values and her impact on others
- Language: Lots of unfamiliar vocabulary: succotash, (Cadillac) fins, house dresses, wringer washing machine.
- Structure: Text is nonlinear; not a problem/solution structure

Challenges for students reading this text:

N/A without knowledge of the particular class

Learning Points From the First Close Reading

- A mental image of the setting—time and place
- Understanding of Gram as a person and what was important to her
- The way Gram interacted with other people
- The meaning of "She Was THAT Kind of Lady" and its connection to a theme about Gram as a generous, kind, simple woman

---

Approaching the Text

____ Teacher reads entire text aloud first, then goes back and reads chunk by chunk

____ Students read entire text first for a general impression; then the teacher reads chunk by chunk

__X__ Teacher reads by chunk without an initial read-through by either the teacher or the students

__X__ **I have determined appropriate text chunks: places to pause and ask questions.**

Chunking the Text

I "prechunked" this text and numbered the portions for easy reference and logical stopping points. While most texts will not include this convenient feature, think of this as a guide to defining *short chunks*.

You should now feel better prepared to "prepare for close reading." In reality, you never feel completely prepared for any new instructional initiative before you jump in and try it and find out for yourself that it actually *does* work and you *can* do it. Considering the following questions—with your professional learning community, a colleague, or on your own—will help solidify some of your thinking about this before we move on to how we will support readers before, during, and after close reading.

Reflecting on What We Know

1. What do you think about this shift away from very focused teaching (one small objective at a time), to a greater emphasis on the meaning of whole text: Is this a good idea? Bad idea? Discuss your thinking.

2. What kinds of evidence do you typically have students look for as they read? What other kinds of evidence suggested in this chapter will help move your students toward deeper knowledge of a text?

3. What do you see as the challenges of a rigorous close reading agenda for students? What are the challenges for teachers?

4. What is one thing you could try tomorrow (or soon) to prepare lessons more aligned with close reading? How about a long-term goal? Share your ideas.

5. Using the same text you selected in Chapter 2, fill in the boxes on the blank Preparing for Close Reading template with work spaces (see Appendix I and the book's website at **www.corwin.com/closerreading**) for Learning Points From the First Close Reading and Approaching the Text.

6. What was hard about doing the work in Number 5 above? What was easy? What questions do you have? If possible, share and discuss your work here with another colleague who is also working on close reading.

Supporting Readers *Before* Close Reading

Instructional Shift

Shorter preread

Before the Common Core	With the Common Core
Scaffolding before reading: "Prereading" was a significant lesson component with many minutes devoted to getting students ready to read through heavy teacher guidance.	**Scaffolding before reading:** The "prereading" part of the lesson is substantially reduced. It is intended to take less time, with less teacher input and more student independence.

The Instructional Shift

With a clearer view of the intent of our close reading lessons and the way we will need to organize for action, we can move on to teaching the lesson itself, beginning with support for students *before* close reading. The scaffolding teachers are now advised to provide—or not provide—for this part of the lesson to prepare students for close reading has caused much angst, more angst perhaps than any other instructional shift suggested by the authors of the Common Core. We have been carefully taught in our preservice college courses, through our graduate studies, through the teacher's manuals that accompany core programs, and by reading professional journal articles that getting ready to read is the most critical component of the reading process, especially for students who struggle with reading. Of course, preparing to read remains a vital component of the reading process, but the *way* we approach it for close reading includes some startlingly different practices.

Limiting Prereading Time

At the exact moment David Coleman (one of the architects of the Common Core and a founder of Student Achievement partners) proclaimed, along with coauthor Susan Pimentel, that students need to get their information from the *text*, not from the *teacher* (Coleman & Pimentel, 2011, p. 6), apparently every educator in the universe was listening. There was an almost immediate outcry: *What about my special needs students? What about primary students? What about English language learners? What about any student who lacks prior knowledge?* Coleman and Pimentel ultimately softened their initial edict (Coleman & Pimentel, 2012, p. 8). But frankly, I don't think they needed to do that.

In Coleman and Pimentel's defense, I seriously doubt that they meant that we should never address the prereading needs for any of our students. What I expect they meant was that we need to reconsider the kinds of support we provide—and for whom—and for how long. Try to envision a reading lesson, perhaps in a third-grade class, based on the picture book *All the Colors of the Earth* (Sheila Hamanaka). This is an incredibly lyrical text that celebrates the diversity of children throughout the world through glorious, poetic images ("love comes in cinnamon, walnut, and wheat . . .") and illustrations that are every bit as delightful as the language.

Now, consider this prereading lesson:

Teacher: "Look at the title. What do you think this book will be about?"

A student: "Colors."

[You think to yourself: *Not really.* The titles of lots of books are misleading, and this is one of those misleading ones. A few other students are frantically waving their hands and chime in with equally off-base ideas. This is going nowhere. Not wanting to pursue this faulty reasoning any longer, you change direction.]

Teacher: "Look at the picture. Now what do you think this book might be about?"

Another student: "I think it's about kids flying on a bird. They're probably going to someplace magical like the end of the rainbow with lots of colors."

[Nice try. The cover illustration shows some smiley children clinging to an eagle in flight, wings extended. But no, this story isn't about kids flying away to a magical rainbow land. Predicting before reading is frequently an unproductive guessing game because readers don't yet have enough information to make reasonable hypotheses. The next *before-reading* element often finds its way into your conversation before you even invite it.]

A student: "I have a connection. I saw a bird like that at a nature center near my aunt's house. There were lots of kinds of birds there."

Another student: "Once a big bird, I'm not sure if it was *that* kind of big bird, flew into our picture window and broke its neck."

[This leads to numerous follow-up questions from classmates: "Did the bird die?" "Could it fly again?" "Did the window break?" At this point, the book itself is a distant memory. You try to refocus the discussion by suggesting a picture walk.]

Although it's unlikely that students would be able to use the pictures in this book to anticipate the story accurately, we know too well that sometimes we do have a student who figures out the storyline just from the pictures—ruining the surprise for everyone else. This is a teacher's worst nightmare as much of the joy of reading comes from discovering for oneself what the text has to offer—and feeling quite clever that you've unlocked the meaning without help.

Meanwhile, as students predict correctly or incorrectly and make personal connections only marginally related to the text, valuable minutes tick by. "Just one more thing," we tell them. "Let's talk about these new words. . . ."

And then we wonder why they have trouble determining meaning from context.

I share this example to show that precious instructional time was wasted—despite our best intentions—when reading programs and distorted practice overemphasized the prereading phase and prereading connections.

Some teachers tell me that it's those personal connections and predictions that get kids interested. Bring them on! I say. If students have some background knowledge about the topic or the author, before reading is the perfect time to summon it up for better comprehension. If you, the reader, want to predict, do that too—but silently, in your head as *real* readers do.

These long, drawn-out prereading lessons can take upwards of half an hour. Most core programs driven by one of those hefty anthologies spend the entire first day of a lesson sequence on prereading. No eyes on print until Day 2. Over the course of a week, that's 20 percent less reading. Multiply that over a year, and this is a serious number of lost literacy minutes.

So what *should* we do?

How to Support Readers Before Close Reading

Appraise Your Text—Honestly

First, carefully examine the text to determine whether students can, in fact, get the information they need from the author—without your doing all the heavy lifting for them. You need to be honest with yourself about this. We are so programmed to think that students need all kinds of background knowledge that we overdo it. To understand *Mercedes and the Chocolate Pilot* (Margot Theis Raven), students really don't need extensive background on the Berlin Airlift, World War II, or postwar Germany; the author provides just the right amount of information within the story itself to make these concepts come alive. Similarly, you don't need to preteach basic geology concepts before reading *How to Dig a Hole to the Other Side of the World* (Faith McNulty). Explaining basic information about the layers of the earth is the purpose of this text. The author does a much better job of describing this in kid-friendly language than I ever could.

However, when particular words or ideas are not easy to understand based on the text alone, that's when we need a game plan. How will we address those complex points, and should we address them *before* reading or as they come up *during* reading? Even more complicated is deciding *who* in our class needs these extra supports. If just your English learners or some other subgroup is likely to require more frontloading, those are the only students who should receive the help. Collaborate with your ESL teacher or your special education teacher or your reading specialist. Communication among professional staff will help students thrive in close reading.

One piece of information that I always want students to consider before reading is geographical location, where the story or informational piece is set if it's a distant country or city. Sometimes you can't determine this at the outset, but other times the location is named right in the title: *Mama Panya's Pancakes: A Village Tale From Kenya* (Mary Chamberlin and Rich Chamberlin) or *Earthquake! A Story of Old San Francisco* (Kathleen Kudlinski). When we talk about the important words in the title, I remind students that they should always, always pay attention to where a story or news article takes place, especially if it isn't a location they recognize or someplace they can readily find on a map. "If it's not someplace you know, then pay really close attention as you read to any clues the author provides about setting or location! Knowing where a story or event takes place will help you understand it better."

Release Responsibility—Gradually

It's sometimes a tough call, deciding whether to frontload information or not. On the one hand, I'm tempted to pull down the world map and jab my finger right on Kenya: "Look, there it is . . . right on the equator . . . in the eastern part of Africa." (And to be totally truthful, sometimes this is exactly what I do—because I just can't help myself.) But on the other hand, will students be able to use a map or other resources on test day—or when their teacher is not around? At the very least, we should be cautious about offering supports in our instruction that students will not also have access to on high-stakes reading assessments. "I don't know why these students got such low scores on this test," teachers have often lamented to me. "They do so well in class. But then comes the Big Test and the results are dismal."

From my vantage point, it's pretty easy to see why there is this teaching-testing disconnect. The teaching provides round after round of guided practice with the same level of teacher support day after day with no gradual release to independence. Then along comes the test, and students are completely on their own. It's a bit like dropping them off a cliff. And without wings to keep themselves aloft, many of them unfortunately crash-land. If our mission isn't to provide students with a lot of our own knowledge, how then, shall we help them survive close reading? We can teach them to support themselves.

Frontload Strategies—Not Knowledge

We need to make the distinction between *teacher* frontloading and students supporting *themselves*. We are definitely not saying that readers should rush headlong into a text, no thinking needed. Rather, we need to teach students the strategies they can use *independently* to successfully approach a text.

We need to teach students the strategies they can use independently to successfully approach a text.

What do *you* do as a reader before reading a book? In the flash of an eye, you glance at the front cover, read the title (does it sound interesting?), check the author's name (one you like, don't like, don't know), and linger for a second over the cover illustration (any guns or blood: reject); maybe you flip the book over to get a brief idea of the content and see what the critics have to say or open to the first page or some other page to see if you get a positive first impression of the author's writing style (a little humor here: bonus). That's about it. Other than on Amazon, I do my best book shopping in airports. Even with limited time to spare, I can duck into one of those little Cover 2 Cover kiosks, apply this quick review strategy to a dozen or more books, purchase one of them, and generally get to my gate before I hear my name called over the loudspeaker.

So what strategies should we teach our students so they can quickly appraise a book too? As we noted in the last chapter, close reading begins with careful observation. And it's important to be clear about the *purpose* right from the get-go. When the close reading involves a picture book, the process looks something like this:

Me:	[holding up the picture book *The Raft* by Jim LaMarche] "This is the book we're going to read today. Our purpose will be to read it closely so we can understand as much about it as possible."
Me:	"What should we pay attention to here to get ourselves ready to read?"
Students:	"The title, the illustration, the names of the author and illustrator."
Me:	"Let's begin with the title: What do you think are the most important words?" [With only two words, this isn't much of

a challenge.] "OK, now look at the word *raft*. What do you notice about it?"

A student:	"It's big. It's got all capital letters. It's bright red."
Me:	"So why might the author have written it that way?"
A student:	"If it's the only important word, and it's written really big, it must be super important."
Me:	"Good thinking. The author is telling us that the *raft* is going to be really important to this story. So how should that make a difference to our reading?"
A student:	"We should look for details about the raft and how it fits into the story?"
A student:	"But I don't know what a raft is."
Another student:	"I know what a raft is. It's—"
Me:	[before the "helpful" student provides the answer] "If you know what a raft is, this is a great time to be thinking about your 'raft' prior knowledge. But if you don't have any prior knowledge, what should you do? Are there any other clues on the cover that can help you?"
Same student who didn't know what a raft was:	"There's a picture. But I'm still not sure."
Me:	"That happens sometimes. So now what? Should you panic?"

[They can tell the answer to this is supposed to be "no" but aren't quite sure where this conversation is going.]

Me:	"If the title is *The Raft*, do you think the author will let you know what a raft is inside the book?" [Heads nod in agreement.] "Then you need to be extra good observers as you read so you pick up every clue."
Me:	"Any other clues to meaning here?"
Student:	"There's a boy in the picture. . . . So we should see how he fits into the story, too."
Me:	"Do you think we're ready to read?"
Students:	"Yes."
Me:	"Wait! One more thing: Does this text look like it will be literary or informational?"

Making the switch from *fiction* and *nonfiction* to *literary* and *informational* to describe text is a bit of a hassle since both students and teachers are so programmed to use the decades-old former (*fiction-nonfiction*) terminology. However, the

Common Core has dictated that we revise the way we label text types. While I still occasionally catch myself reverting to the old labels, I have to admit that the new ones are better because they're more precise regarding a book's primary purpose (most memoir, for example, is factually accurate, situating it within the "informational" category, although the format is literary rather than expository, typical of most nonfiction).

Me: Does this book look like it's going to be *literary*, telling a *story* about a raft? Or does it look like it's going to give us *information*, like how to build a raft?

In this case, it was pretty clear that this was going to be a *story* with characters, a setting, and a problem that led to an outcome. It's critical to get to this question before reading because recognizing the probable text type establishes an organizational framework in students' minds. If the text is literary (a story), they know to look for story parts and themes. If it's informational, they know to look for main ideas and supporting details.

It's important to be clear about the purpose for reading right from the get-go.

Depending on the text, you may be able to ask a follow-up question here, even before reading: "What is the genre?" If they have a strong understanding of various genres and can answer this question, students will have an even more specific structural focus to guide their understanding. (Genre characteristics will need to be specifically taught before students can reliably determine a text's genre. See Chapter 6 for more about how and when to address genre.)

Although they likely won't be able to pin down the genre of *The Raft* at this point, you can still easily ask this question because the picture on the cover looks real, showing a boy about the age of a fourth grader, standing on a raft surrounded by small animals. Students hypothesize that it could be a memoir or realistic fiction or even a biography.

"I guess we'll have to reserve judgment about the genre until we've finished reading," I advise. "Think about the characteristics of different genres as we read this, and I bet you'll be able to figure it out."

That's it, the entire prereading part of the lesson for a picture book—no longer than a couple of minutes. Let's think about what *didn't* happen here:

- I didn't give away anything about this book that the students could get from the reading itself.

- I didn't even supply information about a raft to the child who admitted she didn't know what a raft was. I had examined this book closely enough beforehand to know that the author is going to answer that question very capably inside the cover.

- We didn't get off track on a big conversation about who had ever ridden on a raft.

- We didn't try to invent a plausible storyline based on the cover illustration or a picture walk.

- I didn't confirm or disconfirm their hypothesis about the genre; I just reminded them how to uncover this answer for themselves as they read.
- We didn't list unfamiliar words from the text and talk about their meanings (although there are plenty of great words in this book from which to choose); we will address them during the reading itself.

What I did in place of all these traditional before-reading moves was to name the *purpose* for today's reading and help students by reinforcing the clues available to them so they would know how to focus their thinking once we started reading—as well as when they are reading on their own in the future:

- Notice the important words in the title and anything special about the way those words are written.
  - o Why might the author or illustrator have written them that way?
  - o What might you look for in the text related to the title?
- Notice details within the illustration.
  - o Recognize that the illustrator included those details for a reason. It is our job as readers to figure out that reason while we read.
  - o What might we look for in the text related to the illustration?
- Identify the probable text structure (story with a problem and a solution).
- Consider possible genres.

Notice that all this before-reading support directed students to get the information they need from the text.

Notice that all this before-reading support directed students to get the information they need from the *text*. Our goal for students is that they learn to ask *themselves* these questions without prompting from the teacher. If we begin to focus our scaffolding in this way and are consistent in this approach, students will learn to strategize in a similar manner, taking on an active role in their own reading process. This is a more effective strategy than sitting there passively, waiting for their teacher to offer up the information.

A Case for Using Picture Books

The model lesson above, which demonstrates the use of a picture book for close reading, may strike a chord of disharmony with teachers who argue that with picture books, it's the *teacher* who is doing the reading, not the students. True. But what we're teaching here are the *processes* involved in close reading, demonstrating to students what readers do when they read closely. Complex picture books can be a wonderful tool in this regard because despite the challenges of their meaning, structure, and language, the illustrations help to make the text engaging and provide clues that can aid comprehension. Even struggling students gain access to the content because they are not sidelined by poor decoding skills or lack of fluency. With this up-close view of the way close reading looks and feels, students are better equipped to take the same strategies into their own reading—which of course they will need to do if close reading is ultimately going to help them become college and career ready.

Getting Ready For Independent Close Reading

There will be many occasions when we want students to apply close reading strategies in a text that *they* read, though that reading may be heavily guided by the teacher. Some of these texts will be books; others will be duplicated pages, courtesy of your school's copy machine. When students have their own copy of a text and are expected to read it with their own eyes, they need to learn how to do several more things before they begin.

They need to know how to track meaning. This may involve a system of using sticky notes, margin notes, highlighting, underlining, note taking—or whatever works for today's text. We have much work to do around note taking. (Many students think *everything* they read is important and should be included in their "notes.") We should also help students find a way of tracking meaning when their text is on the computer, since our Common Core assessments will be delivered via online texts.

They need a means of monitoring their understanding. This should include learning the following:

- How to develop quick summaries for brief portions of texts
- How to create gist statements
- How to note important words
- How to paraphrase sentences and paragraphs

These are all skills that need to be modeled and practiced over and over again.

They need to know how to locate appropriate pausing points where they stop and think. Sometimes we forget that this is something we actually need to teach students how to do. When we're teaching with a picture book, or even in a directed lesson where students read the text themselves part by part, *we* choose the stopping points. We know what will be manageable and where the logical breaks occur. It will often be harder for students to determine these natural breaks because they won't have read the text previously (as hopefully you have done before teaching the lesson). But they should learn how to figure out what size chunk works best for them.

They need a strategy for dealing with hard words. Words can be hard because they are difficult to pronounce or difficult to understand. All the same strategies we've suggested to students all along are the ones we want to teach here, too. One exception might be that we should place more emphasis on simply teaching them how to *find* the hard words in an initial close reading. This sense of word awareness will be a good place to begin when we revisit the text for deeper examination.

They need to know how to make use of structural clues. We think of these most readily for informational text: headings, bolded words, bulleted lists, glossaries, and the like. But there are also points to recognize in literary text and poetry:

- If there are chapters, are there titles?

- Are the chapters long or short?

- Are there columns? (How do columns help us as readers?)

- Are there stanzas? (And do students know this term?)

- Is it an excerpt? (What challenges does an excerpt pose?)

We need to teach students how to recognize and make use of these structural elements to help them determine meaning.

They need to think about their reading rate. Does this look like a text that can be read quickly (easy fiction), or is it likely to be complex, requiring a much more methodical approach? For close reading with complex text, the rate will almost always have to be REALLY SLOWLY AND CAREFULLY.

You won't usually be *teaching* the skills listed above during the prereading portion of your lesson. These will require more time than that and are good topics for minilessons aimed at helping students achieve independence through close reading. This topic is addressed more thoroughly in Chapter 7, Moving Students Toward Independence in Close Reading.

Figure 4.1, Ready for Close Reading, provides a list of prereading questions and strategies, including those described above, that you might want to post in your classroom as a quick reference guide for students as they learn *how* to prepare themselves for reading.

Figure 4.1

Ready for Close Reading

- What is my purpose for today's reading?

- What useful information can I get from the title and cover illustration to help me as I read? (Important words? Details in the picture?)

- Does this text look like it's *probably* literary or informational? What makes me think this?

- If it's literary what do I expect to find?

- If it's informational what do I expect to find?

- Can I tell anything about the genre? What genre characteristics could I look for?

- What do I know about this topic?

- Do I know anything about this author?

- Are there pictures or other graphics that will help me understand? How?

- How will I keep track of my evidence?

- How will I make sure I understand as I read?

- Where should I stop to check my understanding (a few checkpoints)?

- Does it look like there might be some hard words? How will I handle hard words?

- Is there anything about the way the author has organized this text that will make it easier (or harder) to read? (Maybe there are bold words, subheadings, a table of contents, graphics, etc.)

- Will I need to read this text slowly in order to understand it, or does it look pretty easy? Why?

Which "Ready to Read" point(s) above look the most helpful for this text? Why?

Available for download at **www.corwin.com/closereading**

When OUR *BEFORE READING INSTRUCTION* Goes Off Track

I anticipate three potential issues that could cause prereading instruction to go off track.

1. Too little frontloading instead of too much frontloading. Taken literally, some teachers see the alternative to "too much" as *none*! I guess that would mean handing a text to a kid and saying "Good luck!" Never mind that the text is really hard. Never mind that the student has no sense of how this piece of literature or source of information fits into the curriculum. Never mind that she's had almost no experience with close reading. Close reading is not intended to be a game of "gotcha." We want our students to succeed. But we want them to succeed outside the classroom as well as in the classroom. This means we have to help them help themselves to be *strategic* readers.

What about those students who really can't make it without a little extra support from us? Should we offer essential prior knowledge that most students have but a few lack? Should we explain words critical to comprehension that we know are missing from some students' vocabularies? We should absolutely provide support to these students. To do less is indeed a poor reflection on our professional judgment. But we need to be much more selective about who gets the help, what kind of help, for how long, and by whom. Support personnel such as ELL teachers, special education teachers, reading specialists, and others need to understand the intent of close reading just as classroom teachers need to understand it so they can be partners in this close reading process.

2. Beginning each lesson with the same prompts every day. It will frustrate teachers and students alike if we're not proactive about actually *teaching* the strategies students will need for close reading. You don't want to have to ask the same questions every day: "What should we look at on the cover? What are the important words in the title? How can the illustration help us?" If students aren't proficient with these strategies, the questions go on and on until you are finally satisfied that students are mentally prepared for the task ahead. Although this isn't quite the same as frontloading content, it is also not very independent. Your goal is to hold up a picture book or distribute a text and lead only with something basic like, "Well now, what shall we do with a text like this?" Eventually, we hope that our students will be the ones to lead *us*.

3. Reverting to past practices. Old habits die hard. Even if we fully subscribe to this new notion of less frontloading, we may find ourselves providing prereading support the "old" way. The questions we ask and the way we approach the text may have become nearly automatic. Sometimes our before-reading instruction will veer off track even when we don't mean for it to do so. We need to keep reminding ourselves that it's "out with the old, in with the new."

Applying What We Know

Completing the *Before Reading* Part of Our Close Reading Plan

With the guidelines we've established for meaningful prereading instruction, filling in the first part of the Preparing for Close Reading is simple and quick (two of our favorite teacher words). This portion of the lesson is noted in Figure 4.2, Planning for Close Reading, the section labeled Before Reading (for a blank version, see Appendix I and the book's companion website at **www.corwin.com/closerreading**). In the next section, I explain each planning component in greater detail for clarification.

Figure 4.2

Planning For Close Reading

(Sample Template)

Text: "She Was *THAT* Kind of Lady"

Purpose: Deep understanding of the text

Before Reading

Clues based on cover illustration—or . . . :

N/A

Clues based on page layout (columns, stanzas, bolded words, etc.):

- The text is broken into parts that are numbered (shows how much to read at one time; where to pause to think)

Clues based on title, author:

- *Was* lets you know this is in the past; It sounds like this lady is no longer living
- Notice the word *lady*—so this must be about a woman, a grown-up
- Notice the word *THAT* is written in all capital letters and it's in italics, so it must be important too.
- When you say someone is *that* kind of boy or *that* kind of girl you usually have some trait or behavior in mind that you're referring to; Look for *"that"* behavior or trait for this lady

Probable text type (literary or informational), possible genre:

- No clues to indicate this is informational, so it's probably literary; can't tell the genre

---

Available for download at **www.corwin.com/closerreading**

Considerations For Close Reading Instruction: Before Reading

Purpose: Deep understanding of the text: Even if you've done close reading dozens of times already, it's still good to take the few seconds needed to clarify the purpose of this lesson. Also, remember that you don't want students to just assume this purpose because when you come back to the text for rereading, you will probably have a more specific objective. The purpose of your close reading will be different on different days.

Clues based on cover illustration: You can ignore this for "She Was *THAT* Kind of Lady" because there isn't a cover. There isn't a picture or any kind of visual. While I'm tempted to add a photograph so readers can get an accurate view of Gram, I also like the idea that without a picture, readers can create their own image—supported by evidence in the text, of course. Sometimes I think that the way we imagine a character makes the story more meaningful.

Clues based on page layout (columns, stanzas, bolded words, etc.): The layout of this text is helpful—parts that are numbered with spaces between them. This will make it easy to highlight individual sentences: *Go to the first sentence in paragraph four* . . . It also makes it clear to students how big a chunk they will be expected to process at one time, though during reading, chunks may be further deconstructed into smaller bites—sentences and phrases and even individual words.

You'll want to point out these structural features to students so that they can make the most efficient use of them—and know to look for them in other texts as well. Again, we are working toward independence. In the past, when I've taken the time to ask children about why an author might have left spaces between paragraphs or portions of a text and how this can help them as readers, I have gotten a lot of blank stares. Hopefully, our shift toward teaching for student independence will change this.

Clues based on title, author: Identifying the word *lady* as important will be easy, though still one that should be pointed out; this person is probably not a young girl. You could also, depending on how deeply you want to get into this, introduce the idea that the author could have used the word *woman*. Why might the author have chosen the word lady instead? What does this imply?

Don't forget *was*. We might not typically pay much attention to this, but it appears this lady is no longer living. That could be important.

Most important of all: *THAT*. The author definitely wants us to pay attention to this word. It's written in both all capitals and italics. Practice reading the title placing the emphasis on this word. Ask students to think about when they might emphasize this word in this way. You want them to see that they most likely have a character trait or behavior in mind: For example, she was a bully; she was *that* kind of girl. Or he practiced layup shots until he got them right; he was *that* kind of kid. We should be able to figure out as we read this text what *that* behavior or trait was that defined this lady.

I would skip attention to the author in this case, because there will be no name recognition. If, on the other hand, the author is someone students recognize, it pays to pause, encouraging them to consider that prior knowledge: Think about what you know about this author's style, the way she develops characters, the way he elaborates on details, the way she uses language.

Probable text type (literary or informational), possible genre: There's not much to go on here with regard to the text type or the genre. Without any of the characteristic informational text features like bolded words, headings, and the like, it's reasonable to conclude that this is probably not an informational text—at least in the usual sense of that term. Depending on students' prior knowledge of genre, you could use the title to point out that this could be a made-up story—either realistic fiction or fantasy. But it could also be a *true* story of a lady—which would change the genre. This could be a good opportunity to broaden students' thinking to also consider memoir or biography. You would want to circle back to this teaching point after reading to confirm.

Although the before-reading part of the lesson is not long, you can see that it addresses components of the text that are much more nuanced than the kinds of things we may have addressed in the past. You will see that this very detailed analysis continues throughout the during-reading part of the lesson, too. Before moving to that, consider the following questions—with your professional learning community, a colleague, or on your own.

Reflecting on What We Know

1. Before reading this chapter, what was your point of view about this shift away from prereading support? What is your point of view now?

2. Sometimes old habits are really hard to break. Which past practice(s) will be the most difficult for you to change? Why? How can you monitor your before-reading instruction to stay on track with this part of the close reading process?

3. Look at the Figure 4.1, Ready for Close Reading. Which of these questions are your students already fairly proficient at answering? Which ones will you need to teach them *how* to answer? How could you support your students in using some of the strategies more effectively?

4. Using the same text you selected and used in Chapters 2 and 3, now plan just the before-reading part of your lesson. Use the blank Preparing for Close Reading template that you can find in Appendix I or on the book's companion website at **www.corwin.com/closerreading**.

5. What was hard about the above task? What was easy? What questions do you have about designing this part of your lesson? If possible, share and discuss your work here with another colleague who is also working on close reading.

CHAPTER 5

Supporting Readers *During* Close Reading

Instructional Shift	
Before the Common Core	With the Common Core
Scaffolding during reading: During reading, students mostly retrieved evidence from the text in support of the lesson objective (finding details about character traits, theme, etc.).	**Scaffolding during reading:** During close reading, students observe and analyze as much as they can about the text to understand how all text elements work together.

The Instructional Shift

What happens during reading is the heart of close reading. This is when we provide the guidance and hold students accountable to all the deep understanding we've been building toward—deep understanding of the whole text, that is, not just evidence that supports one element of the text. That is the shift, and it's a big one. But an even bigger shift is HOW: *How* will we guide students toward this full range of meaning in a text?

Begin With Text-Dependent Questions

Text-dependent questions are directly related to the text. This does not mean just literal-level questions.

One effective and efficient place to start is with text-dependent questions. If we ask questions grounded firmly in the text, students will need to respond with answers grounded in textual evidence. As teachers, we ask *lots* of questions, so we think we're already pretty good at this. But the Common Core has something more in mind that will hold us to an even higher standard in our questioning practices.

It seems simple enough: Text-dependent questions are *directly* related to the text. This does *not* mean just literal-level questions, however. It *does* mean that we need to stop asking questions that students can answer without reading. The question may, in fact, be a great question. But if it doesn't require evidence from the text, it is not a good *reading* comprehension question.

For example, after reading a story about Japanese internment camps following World War II, we ask, "What were some of the hardships faced by Japanese-Americans in these camps?" That question, though literal, is text dependent because the details for answering it come right from the reading. We ask, "Do you think Japanese-Americans in internment camps were treated fairly?" Although this question requires inference, the text supplies the evidence on which the inference can be based, so this question too is text dependent.

We ask, "Do you think internment camps would ever be used in our country today as a means of containing people?" This is a thoughtful question and could be interesting for students to debate. But it is not really text dependent. Answering this question would require lots of world knowledge beyond what was available in this text, most likely demanding some additional research. In the absence of that, students would likely fall back on their gut feeling with hardly a thought toward any kind of textual evidence. We need to remind ourselves about this distinction between *good* questions and good questions that are also *text dependent*. Using that same question—Do you think internment camps would ever be used in our country today as a means of containing people?—might work well *after* an initial close reading and perhaps in the context of another, short text about detainment centers today so that students can ground their thinking in text based on their own research.

Linking Text-Dependent Questions to Standards

There is another important reminder to heed, too. Remember that this is the Age of the Common Core. If we want our students to meet these standards through close reading—and for students to grasp a full range of meaning from the texts they read—we need to pose text-dependent questions linked to a full range of Common Core comprehension standards.

This requires a basic understanding of the standards. But *which* standards? There are a lot of Common Core English Language Arts standards. Which ones will be the most powerful for close reading?

What we would look at in the Standards document and call *comprehension* has been labeled "College and Career Readiness Standards for Reading" (sending a clear message about how the Common Core defines "ready for college"). Regardless, it is this set of standards we need for our text-dependent questions.

The College and Career Readiness (CCR) Anchor Standards Made Simple

There are ten College and Career Readiness (comprehension) "anchor" standards that apply across grade levels K–12, with a benchmark for each grade. These same standards apply to both literary and informational text. They are neatly divided into groups of three under three headings:

- Key Ideas and Details
- Craft and Structure
- Integration of Knowledge and Ideas

One lone standard in a category of its own at the end addresses text complexity:

- Range of Reading and Level of Text Complexity

When you assess students' proficiency in achieving the Common Core, you want to pay attention to the grade-level benchmarks for each anchor standard. But for instructional purposes, what is most important are the "big ideas" in the anchor standards themselves. Table 5.1, with information taken directly from the Common Core State Standards official website, identifies these College and Career Readiness Anchor Standards for Reading.

What I have noticed as I've traveled to districts talking about the Common Core is that teachers are not as familiar with these standards as they could be. If I asked you to identify Standard 4 or Standard 6 or any of these standards, would you, without hesitation, be able to do it without referencing the chart? Until we have a working knowledge of these standards, it will be difficult for us to use them easily to support and guide our close reading. I can help you remember them more easily by offering a key word or phrase for each one (see Figure 5.1). (You might want to find your pen at this point to jot these words and phrases on Table 5.1.)

Standard 1: Finding evidence

Standard 2: Theme, main idea, summary

Standard 3: Story parts, facts, details

Standard 4: Vocabulary (word choice)

Standard 5: Structure, genre, syntax

Standard 6: Point of view, purpose

Standard 7: Different kinds of texts

Standard 8: Critiquing text

Standard 9: Text-to-text connections

Standard 10: Text complexity

Table 5.1

College and Career Readiness Standards for Reading

	Key Ideas and Details
1	Read closely to determine what the text says explicitly and to make logical inferences from it; cite specific textual evidence when writing or speaking to support conclusions drawn from the text.
2	Determine central ideas or themes of a text and analyze their development; summarize the key supporting details and ideas.
3	Analyze how and why individuals, events, and ideas develop and interact over the course of a text.
	Craft and Structure
4	Interpret words and phrases as they are used in a text, including determining technical, connotative, and figurative meanings, and analyze how specific word choices shape meaning or tone.
5	Analyze the structure of texts, including how specific sentences, paragraphs, and larger portions of the text (e.g., a section, chapter, scene, or stanza) relate to each other and the whole.
6	Assess how point of view or purpose shapes the content and style of a text.
	Integration of Knowledge and Ideas
7	Integrate and evaluate content presented in diverse media and formats, including visually and quantitatively, as well as in words.
8	Delineate and evaluate the argument and specific claims in a text, including the validity of the reasoning as well as the relevance and sufficiency of the evidence.
9	Analyze how two or more texts address similar themes or topics in order to build knowledge or to compare the approaches the authors take.
	Range of Reading and Level of Text Complexity
10	Read and comprehend complex literary and informational texts independently and proficiently.

Source: English Language Arts Standards, Anchor Standards, College and Career Readiness Anchor Standards for Reading (2010c). Copyright © 2010 National Governors Association Center for Best Practices and Council of Chief State School Officers. All rights reserved.

Figure 5.1

A Quick Way to Remember The Common Core Anchor Standards

1. Standards 1 through 3 (Key Ideas and Details) revolve around this:

   WHAT is the author saying?

   All these standards relate to the essential *meaning* in the text.

2. Standards 4 through 6 ask students to examine this:

   HOW is the author saying it?

   These standards all deal with how the author is *delivering* the message.

3. And Standards 7 through 9 speak to the following:

   WHY is the author saying it?

   That is, now that you understand the content, why is it important? What will you *do* with the information?

Understanding the Implications of the CCR Standards for Close Reading

To understand the implications of these standards for close reading, we need to probe a little deeper. What is the focus of the Common Core in each of these areas? Let's look at them one at a time.

Standard 1: Evidence. This is the standard through which students monitor their understanding. Throughout close reading, there should be repeated opportunities for "checking in" with questions such as the following:

- What do you know now that you didn't know before?

- What is the first thing that jumps out at you and why?

Questions about basic meaning should also lead to inferences:

- What do you think are the most *important* details in this part of the text? Why?

- What details surprised you? Why?

You will probably notice once you begin creating text-dependent questions aligned to standards that many of them address Standard 1. This worries some teachers because it seems that the thinking for Standard 1 is fairly low level and literal compared to that which students need for Standards 2 through 9. This really is

OK—as a place to begin. It's good to check for basic understanding. But if you have a question that addresses Standard 1, think about a possible follow-up question you could ask that would take students deeper into the text and hence into the more analytical thinking called for in other standards. Rather than asking lots of text-dependent questions that jump from topic to topic, what you really want is a *sequence* of questions where one question leads to the next and each question leads students a bit deeper into the text.

Standard 2: Summary/Theme/Main Idea. The tricky thing about meeting this standard is that now students are expected to produce summaries that incorporate the theme or main idea, showing its development over the course of a text. A sample question might look like this:

- What is the author's message in this story, and how does the author show this through the events that took place?

I like using this question along the way:

- What is this text starting to be about?

This alerts students early on in their reading that they should be thinking about the text's theme or main idea. Too often with theme and main idea, we sort of "spring it" on kids at the end of a text, which is a little late in the game for gathering evidence to support their thinking.

Also noteworthy within this standard is the expectation for paraphrasing. This is a very good thing! When students can put meaning into their own words, we can be more confident that they truly understand what they have read.

Standard 3: Story Parts, Facts, Details. The Common Core emphasizes the *relationship* among elements in a text:

- How does the setting impact the problem?
- How does one event lead to another?
- How do the main character's motivations affect her interaction with other characters?

This raises the bar in an aspect of text study, which has been relatively straightforward in the past.

Standard 4: Vocabulary. The Common Core is more concerned with the *important* words than the *hard* words. This is a very different way of looking at vocabulary: vocabulary as *craft*. Students will now be expected to think about the following:

- **Tone.** The author's choice of particular words and how they shape the tone of the text. For instance, the author might write, "The little boy got off the bus with his report card and trudged home." The tone would be very different if instead the author had written, "The little boy got off the bus with his report card and skipped home."

- **Figurative language.** Students will also be asked to explain the use of figurative language and its impact on meaning: *idioms, similes, metaphors,* and *personification.*

- **Multiple meanings.** Words with multiple meanings require students to determine their meaning from context.

In short: How does the author play with words—in a variety of ways—to add meaning?

Standard 5: Structure, Genre, Syntax. Some aspects of this standard are what we would typically expect, whereas others are more subtle. I've made the case earlier in this book for placing a stronger emphasis on text structure and genre. With or without the Common Core, structure and genre will serve us well in enhancing students' comprehension. But there's more. Remember that this standard falls within the Craft and Structure band. Examining structure as *craft* is a different kind of challenge:

Examining structure as craft is a different kind of challenge.

- How has the author crafted the introduction of the text to get readers' attention?

- Why did the author place this word first in the sentence instead of last, and what effect does that have?

- How does the first stanza of this poem connect to the second stanza?

- Does this passage include description, narration, or argument?

- How does the author vary sentence length and why?

The list goes on. These are also ways that an author plays with language.

Standard 6: Point of View/Purpose. The challenge here, as indicated earlier, is helping students, even young children, understand point of view or purpose—even with informational text. This means examining multiple accounts of the same basic story or situation and seeing how the author's point of view influences the way the story is told or situation is explained. Here are some text selection tips:

- Use primary-source documents. These will be especially useful because they are *informational* in intent—although the format is generally *narrative.* This is different from many informational sources that are organized around main ideas and details with headings, bolded words, and other nonfiction text features.

- For literary text, choose a lot of stories with a first-person narrator. With a first-person narrator, it's obvious whose side of the story you are getting.

- Use the numerous fairy tales that have alternate versions, told from different points of view—children really enjoy these.

- Use nonfiction texts that present flip sides of the same issue. Publishers are beginning to release books that support teaching about opposing points of view based on topics to which intermediate-grade children can relate: Should children play video games? Should children be required to wear school uniforms? Other resources have a "choose your own ending" format where readers make decisions about important historical issues depending on *their* point of view: What should they do next? Then they get to watch how the situation plays out based on the choice they made. (Children *love* these books!)

- Look for literary texts where the story is told by various characters within the story, where different chapters or pages have different narrators. A picture book set up this way is *Voices in the Park* by Anthony Browne. A chapter book with multiple narrators, which children just love, is *Because of Mr. Terupt* by Rob Buyea.

Standard 7: Different Kinds of Texts. The Common Core broadens our definition of *text* beyond words printed on a piece of paper: Internet sites, video, photographs, art prints and illustrations, live performances, even conversations are acknowledged as text. We will see all these text types featured in text-to-text connections in Standard 9. But in order to make connections that are meaningful, students first need to learn to use these sources knowledgeably. That means we have a lot of teaching to do.

For video, students will need to address points such as these:

- How did different images capture your attention?
- What individuals are most often represented in the media, and what individuals (e.g., gender, culture, age) are absent?

For photographs, we may want students to consider questions such as these:

- Based on what you have observed in the photograph, what might you infer or conclude from this image?
- What questions does this image raise in your mind?

I provide lots of additional guidance for supporting multiple text types in Chapter 6 in the section with follow-up tasks for after reading.

Standard 8: Critiquing the Text. Keep in mind that *this applies to informational text only*. Ultimately, we are being asked to teach students to assess a text's validity and reliability by teaching them to ask question such as these:

- Is the information current?
- Does the author present the topic fairly, respecting varying points of view?
- Has information been omitted, leading to bias?

This kind of deep critical appraisal is more the expectation for middle school than elementary school children, but you need to lay the groundwork for future expectations. In Grades 3 through 5, the emphasis is more on verifying that the author is supporting his or her claims with sufficient evidence:

- Which points support which claims?

Notice that work on this standard aligns well with Writing Standard 1: Argument and Opinion Writing.

Standard 9: Text-to-Text Connections. For reasons already discussed, this is the only kind of connection mentioned in the Common Core. In the sample assessments I've seen, students will frequently be asked to synthesize information from multiple sources (three or four or five) as they respond to questions. This is a triple whammy. What will students need to know and be able to do to achieve this?

- They will have to be proficient at reading multiple texts closely, gathering all the necessary meaning from each one.

- They will need to know how to synthesize information and evidence gathered from multiple texts, incorporating useful pieces from each one as needed to respond to whatever questions they are asked.

- And they will need to cite the particular source from which they retrieved each specific piece of information.

With this in mind, our close reading agenda should *always* include at least two texts with a logical connecting point. Think outside the box: An informational piece may work well with a poem. An art print or photograph could support just about any text. Consider connecting themes and big ideas, two versions of the same story, texts on the same topic each with a different focus, and so on. The connection will need to be based on a *significant* textual element, however, not a detail that has little impact on meaning.

Standard 10: Text Complexity. Chapter 2 of this book is devoted to text complexity, so we don't need to discuss the details again here. One final point is that text complexity as a *standard* "works" differently than do all the others. With Standards 1 through 9, we have specific grade-level benchmarks against which to measure students' proficiency with the standard. But Standard 10 mostly defines for us the kind of text students must read in order to address the other standards. It's like apples and oranges, probably the reason it stands alone in its very own "standards band": Range of Reading and Level of Text Complexity.

Our close reading agenda should always include at least two texts with a logical connecting point.

Putting the Standards to Work for Close Reading

I know this seems like a lot of information to absorb—and use. If you are feeling a little overwhelmed here, know that you have plenty of company. Most of us would say we have not received the kind of guidance for Common Core implementation that inspires confidence. But when you see how naturally we are able to meet many of these goals through the text-dependent questions we ask, you may feel that you can actually breathe again.

The following charts will help you. Figure 5.2, Close Reading Questions Aligned to Common Core's College and Career Readiness Anchor Standards for Reading, provides you with questions aligned to each standard. You will see that there are two columns here, one for literary text and the other for informational sources. These questions are intended to show you the *kinds* of questions that would align to different standards.

For an even more extensive list of questions for each standard, check out Leslie Blauman's (2014) *The Common Core Companion: The Standards Decoded, Grades 3–5: What They Say, What They Mean, How to Teach Them.* This spiral-bound resource includes standards-aligned questions by individual grade level, not just for the reading standards but also for writing, speaking and listening, and language. A version with this same title for Grades K–2 teachers by Sharon Taberski (2014) is also available, as are versions for middle and high school teachers by series originator Jim Burke (2103a, 2013b).

The Common Core does not really support "framing questions," those "stock," generic questions we might pose for *any* text as an isolated lesson focus: What is

Figure 5.2

Close Reading Questions Aligned to Common Core's College and Career Readiness Anchor Standards For Reading

Standard	Potential Questions For Literary Text	Potential Questions For Informational Text
1. Finding evidence	• What clues to meaning do you find on the cover (illustration, title, information about the author) that prepare you to read this story? Who is the narrator? • What does the author mean by __? • Identify the characters, setting, problem, outcome. • What do you think are the most important details in this part of the text? Why? • What do you know about the character(s)/problem/setting from this part of the text? • What do you know about the character(s)/problem/setting that you didn't know before? • What did the author want us to know here? How do you know? • What is the first thing that jumps out at you? Why? • What is the next thing that jumps out at you? Why?	• What kind of clues to meaning do you find on the cover (illustration, title, information about the author) that prepare you to read this text? What does the author mean by __? • Who is providing this information? • Identify the topic and main points. • What facts/details really stand out to you? Why? • What do you know about this person/situation/place from this part of the text? • What do you know about this person/situation/place that you didn't know before? • What did the author want you to know here? How do you know? • What is the first thing that jumps out at you? Why? • What is the next thing that jumps out at you? Why?
2. Theme, main idea, summary	• Explain what is happening here in your own words (paraphrase). • What is this story starting to be about? • What is the author's message? • What is the big idea? • What lesson does ___ learn? • What is the author's message, and how does the author show this throughout the story?	• Explain what the author is saying in your own words (paraphrase). • What is this [article] starting to be about? • What did you learn in this part of the text? • What is the main idea? • What is the main idea, and how does the author show this in the text?
3. Story parts, facts	• How does the setting (time and place) make a difference to the story? • How does [character] change throughout the story? • What character trait/feeling is present here? • Why does the author choose these particular details to include?	• How does [person] contribute to this situation/problem (or the solution of the problem)? • How does one event/step lead to the next (cause/effect)? • What are the most important facts/details? • Why does the author choose these particular details to include?

Standard	Potential Questions For Literary Text	Potential Questions For Informational Text
4. Vocabulary/ words*	• What tone or mood does the author create? What words contribute to that tone? • What does this word mean based on other words in the sentence? • What is the meaning of this simile/ personification/idiom/metaphor, and why did the author choose it? • What are the most important words to talk about this text? • What words paint a picture in your mind? • What word did the author choose to add meaning? How do these choices display craft?*	• Why did the author choose this word? • What tone or mood does the author create? What words contribute to that tone? • What does this word mean based on other words in the sentence? • What is the meaning of this simile/ personification/idiom/metaphor, and why did the author choose it? • What are the most important words to talk about this text? • What words paint a picture in your mind? • What word did the author choose to add meaning? How do these choices display craft?*
5. Structure, genre, syntax*	• How does this text "look" on the page (stanzas, illustration, etc.)? How will this support your reading? • What is the structure of this story (or part of the story)? • What is the genre? What genre characteristics do you find? • Are the sentences easy or hard to understand? Why? • Why do you think the author chose this genre or format (like picture book, poem, etc.)? • How does this passage/paragraph fit into the text as a whole? • How does the author craft the organization of this story to add to meaning? • Where does the author want us to use different thinking strategies (picturing, wondering, etc.)? What makes you say this?	• How does this text "look" on the page (columns, numbered paragraphs, etc.)? How will this support your reading? • What is the structure of this text (or part of the text)? • What is the genre? What genre characteristics do you find? • Are the sentences easy or hard to understand? Why? • Why do you think the author chose this genre or format (like picture book, poem, etc.)? • How does this passage/paragraph fit into the text as a whole? • How does the author craft the organization of this [article] to add to meaning? • Where does the author want us to use different thinking strategies (picturing, wondering, etc.)? What makes you say this?
6. Point of view*	• Who is speaking in this passage? • Whom does the narrator seem to be speaking to? • What is the narrator's/character's point of view (what does he or she think about ___)? • What does the narrator/character care about? • Are there particular words that the author chose to show strong feelings? • Do different characters have different points of view about___? • How do you know?	• Who is the author of this article/book? • Whom does the author seem to be speaking to? • What is the author's point of view about ___? • What does the author care about? • Why did the author write this? • Do you think the author is openly trying to convince you of something? What makes you say this? • Does this information change your point of view about __?

(Continued)

Standard	Potential Questions For Literary Text	Potential Questions For Informational Text
7. Different kinds of texts	• How do the illustrations add to the meaning? • How is the [live version, video, etc.] the same or different from the print version?	• How do the graphics [charts, maps, photographs, etc.] add to or clarify the message? • How does the [video, interview, etc.] add to or change your understanding of this subject? • How do you read this like a scientist/ historian?
8. Critiquing text	• This standard is not applied to literary text.	• Did the author provide sufficient evidence on the subject to support his or her claim? • Did the author present the subject fairly, explaining all sides of the situation without bias? • Did the author provide sufficient evidence on the subject? • Did the author leave out information that should have been included? • Is the author knowledgeable on the subject with current information? • Is there anything the author could have explained more thoroughly for greater clarification? What?
9. Text-to-text	• How is [Character 1] the same as or different from [Character 2]? • How is [first story] different from [second story]? • How is the message/theme of [Story 1] the same or different from the message/theme of [Story 2]? • [For stories by the same author] Is there anything about the way [Story 2] was written that reminds you of the craft in [Story 1]? Explain.	• Does the information from [Text 1] express the same or different point of view from Text 2]? • What new information did you get from [Text 2] that was not included in [Text 1]? • Is there anything in [Text 2] that contradicts the information in [Text 1]? What is the contradiction? How could you decide which source is more accurate?

*See separate chart on author's craft, Figure 5.3, Recognizing the Author's Craft During Close Reading.

the theme? What is the narrator's point of view? What trait does this character demonstrate? So when you ask questions about these elements, be sure to customize them for the particular text you are reading, and make sure they are linked to the content of the text itself and to questions probing other standards rather than just to a skill you wish to reinforce with your students.

If you analyze your own questions for a close reading lesson you design, you will probably find that you've done a good job with questions for Standards 1 through 3: Key Ideas and Details. Although we may have to "tweak" our questions in this band a bit to meet all the challenges of the Common Core, we really are very practiced in asking about basic content: evidence, big ideas, and text elements.

But questions for the next band, Craft and Structure, may be spotty (beyond questions about basic word meaning for Standard 4). This is an area where many teachers don't feel particularly strong—identifying the elements of author's craft in text. You may want to advocate for yourself here by pushing for some professional development: What does it mean to "read like a writer?" And how do we bring this knowledge to the children we teach?

The power of close reading will be achieved through the lively interconnection between the teacher and the students and the complex text.

Since this is such a troubling area for many teachers, I've prepared a chart with questions to delve deeper into the author's craft (supporting Standards 4, 5, and 6). See Figure 5.3, Recognizing the Author's Craft During Close Reading.

It is likely that most of your questions that move students into the skills described in Standards 7 through 9, Integration of Knowledge and Ideas, will surface *after* an initial close reading, when you revisit your text to dig deeper. Students need a solid understanding of the content and craft before they can use this knowledge to integrate and synthesize. If you don't see many opportunities for these in your initial lesson, try to find a way to integrate them in a follow-up lesson.

Figure 5.3

Recognizing the Author's Craft During Close Reading

Elements That Contribute to Craft	Possible Questions
Identifying imagery, including comparisons: • **Similes** • **Metaphors** • **Personification** • **Figurative language** • **Symbols**	1. What is being compared? 2. Why is the comparison effective? (typically, because of the clear/strong/unusual/striking/vivid, etc., connection between the two) 3. What symbols are present? Why did the author choose these symbols? 4. Are there lots of symbols? If so, could this be an <u>allegory</u>?
Effective word choice	1. What word(s) stand out? Why? (strong/contrasts to what you expect, vivid) 2. How do particular words get us to look at characters, events, setting, or other text elements in a particular way? 3. Are there any words that seem "old"—words or expressions that you don't hear very much today? What does this show? 4. Did the author use nonstandard English or words from another language? Why? What is the effect? 5. Are there any words that could have more than one meaning? Why might the author have played with language in this way?
Tone and voice	1. What <u>one word</u> describes the tone? (will be something like *funny, serious, angry, lonely*) 2. Is the voice formal or informal? If it seems informal, how did the author make it that way? If it's formal, what makes it formal? 3. Does the voice seem appropriate for the intent of the content?
Structuring the beginning, middle, and end	1. How does the author craft the beginning of the story or informational piece to get readers' attention? 2. How does the author build suspense during the text? 3. How does the author end the piece in a memorable way?
Linking parts of the passage together: • **Phrases** • **Sentences** • **Paragraphs/stanzas**	1. What words link thoughts together? (e.g., *and, but, however, therefore, in conclusion*) 2. What do these linking words show about the ideas in the text? 3. How does the author help you understand how the text is organized?

Elements That Contribute to Craft	Possible Questions
Sentence structure: • **Short sentence** • **Long sentences** • **Sentences where word order is important** • **Sentence fragments** • **Questions** • **Commands** • **Balanced sentences**	1. What stands out about the way this sentence is written? 2. Why did the author choose a **short** sentence here? (short: stands out from sentences around it; for emphasis) 3. Why did the author make this sentence really **long**? (long: may convey the "on and on" sense of the experience; to create rhythm) 4. Why did the author write a **fragment** instead of a complete sentence**?** (emphasis; often shows the internal thought of a character) 5. Based on the **order of the words** in this sentence, which one do you think is the most important? Why? What was the author trying to show by placing this word in this place? (Strong words at the beginning or end of a sentence are more powerful than if the same word is in the middle of the sentence.) 6. Why does the author use a **question** here? (Rhetorical questions are not really intended to be answered, but to make a point: "Why am *I* always the one who gets blamed?" Some questions set up the main idea of the paragraph: "Why do we care about endangered species?") 7. What is the **exclamation point/command** all about? (high importance; bossy tone) 8. What sentences are **balanced** here? Which are intentionally *not* balanced? (Balance creates pleasing rhythm; intentionally out of balance creates a strong effect because you notice the change.) What punctuation does the author use to create balance? (might be a comma, semicolon)
How many types of writing there are in the passage	1. Example: Is there narration, exposition, argument, rhymed lines, description, etc.? 2. How do these different types of writing make the text more lively?
Punctuation and print conventions	1. Is there anything unusual or interesting about the punctuation or the way the author used punctuation? (parentheses to offer small asides; semicolons; etc.) 2. Did the author place print in an interesting way to reinforce meaning? 3. What about font and the size of print? Do these contribute to meaning? How?
Repeated lines, words, or phrases	1. Does the author repeat particular words, lines, or phrases? 2. How does this impact meaning? (provides emphasis)

When OUR DURING-READING INSTRUCTION Goes OFF Track

Three during-reading issues concern me. The first relates to the use of the standards. The second has to do with the use of questions. The third focuses on when we ask our questions.

1. That educators will try to reduce close reading to a formula. I'm beginning to hear from teachers about a means of approaching close reading that I consider ill-advised. Their sources tout an organizational scheme that looks like this: Read a text three times. In the first close reading, address Standards 1 through 3. In the second round, focus on Standards 4 through 6. The third time through a text, examine Standards 7 through 9. This is appealing to teachers because it appears to simplify the process. But it is arbitrary and prescriptive, and it often doesn't work. Don't drink this Kool-Aid.

It is true that in an initial close reading you may focus heavily on Standards 1 through 3. But there will also be many opportunities to apply Standards 4 through 6 that support students' basic construction of meaning. The lesson included in this chapter is a good example of why this system doesn't work: Students will not fully appreciate this text unless you work with vocabulary right away (Standard 4). The fine points of the way the piece is structured (Standard 5) lead students to comprehension, right along with the words themselves. On the other hand, there is no real attention here to Standard 2 (theme) because I've decided that would be too much to cover in this first read-through. Please, please do not try to reduce close reading to a formula. It should *address* the standards, but it should not be *dictated* by the standards; it should be guided by the *text*.

2. That text-dependent questions will be misused. My second concern relates to a possible misuse of questions. A potential hazard is the danger that our wonderful text-dependent questions could find their way into "packets"—page after page of questions that teachers distribute for students to answer in writing. Used in this manner, our questions will no longer be so wonderful. ***The power of close reading is achieved through the lively interconnection between the teacher and the students and the complex text***. Once we remove the teacher from the equation, we reduce close reading to a lonely, frustrating exercise. There is a place for responding to close reading in writing, but this should never take the place of the lesson itself.

3. That we won't ask questions until after reading. My final concern stems from viewing a "close reading" lesson recently on a website reputed to post only resources vetted for their superior quality. This lesson (following a number of prereading transgressions) instructed teachers during reading to "read the text to the class or engage in 'popcorn' reading with different students reading different portions of the text aloud." That was it, all the support students were to receive during the reading itself. Six or seven questions were then listed for ***after reading***—many of which were barely text dependent. Question quality aside, we can't wait to ask questions until ***after*** reading. For "close reading" we need to ask many questions as we move through the text so we can help students tease out bits and pieces of meaning as the author offers them to us. All you really get afterward are questions about the big ideas that tie the text together.

Considerations For Close Reading Instruction: During Reading

Now, let's develop the next stage of our lesson plan. In this section, I will show you the text-dependent questions I would use for each chunk of our text, as well as the standard that aligns with the question.

As I've said before, on a day-to-day basis I would not expect any of us to pick through our questions in this precise way to designate the matching standard. But it's a good exercise on occasion for examining the thoroughness of our questions. The biggest benefit is that it will show us very quickly not just the standards we've covered but which ones we are not addressing. This is the ghost that could haunt us. Congratulations to us for incorporating many good text-dependent questions into our close reading lessons. Some texts will surely be better suited to working toward some standards than others, so we can't expect we will work toward every standard in every lesson. However, if we routinely omit questions that will help students meet certain standards, we are limiting our students' close reading capacity.

Now we are ready to look at the during-reading portion of our lesson plan represented in Figure 5.4 (for a blank version, see Appendix I and the book's companion website at **www.corwin.com/closerreading**). This shows how those standards-based, text-dependent questions can guide students toward deep understanding, even in an initial close reading. Following the lesson plan, there is an explanation of this part of the lesson.

Figure 5.4

Planning for Close Reading

(Sample)

During Reading

*Reading anchor standards are identified in parentheses next to each question

Questions students should ask themselves for each chunk of text:

- What is the author telling me?
- Any hard or important words?
- What does the author want me to understand?
- How does the author play with language to add to meaning?

Follow-up: Text-dependent questions for the teacher to ask about each chunk of text:

First chunk:

- Who is telling this story? (granddaughter) (1)*
- What do you know about this lady so far? (many details provided) (1)
- What does the author want you to understand? (Grandma wasn't "cool," but this doesn't seem to be a bad thing.) (3)
- What strategy do you think the author wants us to use here? Why? (picturing; lots of details to create picture in your mind) (5)

Second chunk:

- What word does the author repeat in the first couple of sentences that stands out? Why do you think the author repeats these words? (plain; plain is a good word to describe Gram) (5)
- What are the details in this section mostly about? (1) (doing the wash)
- Doing the wash isn't very exciting. Why do you think the author spent so much time describing this? (shows that Gram's life wasn't very exciting by most standards; helps us in understanding the time period) (3)
- Does the author seem to be telling the story here from the point of view of a child or an adult? What makes you think this? (child's point of view; long-ago memories) (1)
- What about the last line of this chunk? Are you beginning to understand what *"that"* means? (The author used a line from this chunk as the title; seeing that Gram is a simple and good lady) (5, 2)
- What are you learning in this chunk about Gram's point of view on life? What makes you think this? (didn't need fancy things; liked her old ways) (6)

Third chunk:

- What are you learning about Gram here? (worked in the family grocery store 43 years; gave granddaughter Popsicle) (1)
- What is the author trying to show us here? (Gram's generosity) (3)
- How many people in Gram's life have you met so far? (2—Pop and granddaughter) (1)
  What does it mean to give someone "a hand"? (help them out) (4)

Fourth chunk:

- What is this chunk mostly about? (the food Gram made) (1)
- Why is the word *real* in quotes? (Some people don't consider staying home and cooking a "real" job.) (5)
- What senses does the author want us to use here? (picturing, smelling) (5) What words lead us to these senses? (peaches, roast beef, fried chicken, pickles) (4)
- Any words you don't understand here? (maybe *Victorian, succotash, pie face, chili sauce, lemon meringue*) (4)
- Are you beginning to get a more complete picture of this time and place? Describe it. (3)
- How does this chunk fit with the Chunk 3 above? (both about Gram's hard work and generosity) (5)
- Do you have anything to add for *"that"* kind of lady? (generosity, thoughtfulness) (3)

Fifth chunk:

- What is this section mostly about? (driving) (1)
- Does this change your thinking about Gram? How? (Gram liked to feel special, important; although she mostly fulfilled traditional female roles, she was strong, smart, independent.) (3)
- What words lead you to this new thinking? ("felt like a queen;" Cadillac; perched; guided; didn't mind being alone) (4)

Sixth chunk:

- What is the author giving you information about in this chunk? (1) (Gram and her porch)
- The author uses hyperbole (exaggeration) in this chunk and also in the chunk above. What is getting exaggerated? Why is the author doing this? (longest fins in the world; every problem in the universe—makes the point that the fins were *really* big and there were *lots* of problems (4)
- Does this part confirm anything you already know about *that lady*? Does it add anything new? (confirms *generosity*; adds *friendliness*) (3)

Seventh chunk:

- What details is the author sharing here? (rice pudding, smile) (1)
- What does it mean to "collect people"? (lots of friends) (4)
- Why do you think the author included this information? (She was kind to others, so they were kind to her (6)

(Continued)

(Continued)

Eighth chunk:

- What is happening in this part of the text? (Gram is telling stories to her great granddaughter) (1)

- What interesting punctuation do you see at the beginning of this chunk? What are these called? What is the author trying to show here? (ellipses; showing the passing of time) (5)

- How can you tell time has passed? (little girl now was the great granddaughter) (1)

- Why does the author include these stories (more details about Grams' simple life; hardships; small details that were memorable to her; showed Gram's point of view—that she just accepted that life was like this, even the disappointing parts; she didn't complain) (6)

Ninth chunk:

- What are you finding out here? (granddaughter and family now lived with Gram) (1)

- Why does Gram call herself "the old gray mare"? What is she referring to when she says this? (This refers to the old song lyrics: "The old gray mare, she ain't what she used to be…" Just like the old gray mare, Gram feels old.) (9)

- Again the author repeats the line, "She was *that* kind of lady." What kind of lady is that? (many traits evident by now) (3)

In this part of the text you get a more direct view of the granddaughter's (author's) feelings about her grandmother. What are those feelings and how are these feelings shown? (feels lots of love; moved in to care for her and her house) (2)

Available for download at **www.corwin.com/closerreading**

Applying What We Know

Completing the During-Reading Part of Our Close Reading Plan

I will be honest and confess that completing this part of the planner does take time. Just writing all these questions eats up more than a few minutes. More than that, though, I get stuck in the story. Once I start drilling down and down and down, I find there is so much to uncover that it's hard to pull myself away. But this is not a bad thing. I see the questions I am creating in the faces of the students who will soon sit with me and respond to them. This is my very favorite part of close reading, and I know that if I plan thoughtfully, I will be rewarded many times over with all the satisfaction and appreciation we get when a lesson goes well.

And lots of that reward comes from teachers. The lessons I teach are always in someone else's classroom, with twenty or so students sitting cross-legged on a rug in front of me and maybe half that number of teachers crowded around watching. I know this should make me seriously nervous. But after about the first paragraph, we're somewhere deep inside the text, and the next time I look up, there's so much pride smiling back at me. "Those were *our* kids answering those questions," teachers remind me in the debriefing session afterward. Yes, I know. When you read really, really closely, there's no limit to what you can find in an author's words—even when you're only nine years old.

We can hold our own debriefing session for this part of the lesson right here. Rather than going chunk by chunk, it will be more effective to examine the questions in relation to each standard. You may want to review Figure 5.3 again before engaging in this analysis.

Depending on Standards for Our Text-Dependent Questions

Standard 1. In nearly every chunk, I led with a question or two aimed at checking for basic understanding. These became a springboard to follow-up questions that asked students to think more deeply.

Standard 2. This standard is not directly addressed in this lesson until the final question in the last chunk. This is intentional. I would not plan to delve into theme during the initial reading because you have to understand Gram as a person (a whole day's work in itself) before you can put these clues together to see the message—or multiple messages—about grandmother and granddaughter. I would make this the focus of a follow-up lesson.

Standard 3. There are an abundance of questions in this lesson that will help students meet Standard 3, understanding the interaction among text elements. This makes sense because this is a memoir, and memoirs focus heavily on people and places and the experiences that bring them together. The same evidence used in today's lesson for revealing character could be revisited subsequently for theme.

Standard 4. There are very few "hard" words in this text, the kind that would derail basic construction of meaning. But there are plenty of potentially unknown words and expressions that give you a better appreciation of Gram and appreciation of this time period. This lesson highlights era-specific words like *Victorian*, *Cadillac fins*, and *succotash*. It also focuses on figurative phrases like "give someone a hand" and "pie face."

Standard 5. There are many questions in this lesson related to the skills outlined in Standard 5. While I don't ask students about the overall structure of the text—though this could be useful to discuss in a follow-up lesson on genre—I do focus on small points that ask students to examine the author's craft. Many of these structural

(Continued)

(Continued)

elements are subtle: placement of quotation marks around a particular word, italicized words, repetition of lines, the use of punctuation (in this case ellipses) to convey meaning, places in the text crafted to inspire the use of various comprehension strategies. One reason to highlight these aspects of the writer's craft is to make the link to student writing: "Here's something you could try in your own writing, too."

Standard 6. When I first reviewed my lesson after writing it, I noticed I didn't have any questions that addressed Standard 6. This seemed odd because a memoir should reveal point of view. I went back to the text and looked for places where point of view should be apparent to students. I found two chunks where I would definitely want to insert such a question and added them to my plan. This is the benefit of being familiar with the standards; you will recognize what is present in your lesson and what you have omitted—intentionally or accidentally.

Standards 7–9. The absence of questions addressing these standards is not an accident. There are no graphics that accompany this text, so we can't incorporate a picture or photograph. Although the Common Core includes memoir among its informational text types, a memoir doesn't work for assessing "validity and reliability"; memoir is *supposed* to present a personal perspective. There is one small text connection here (which most children will never recognize). I noted it mostly because of the inference about being an "old gray mare." (I also sang a few bars from the song when I taught this lesson; the kids looked at me as if I were from a different planet.) These kinds of questions would find their rightful place in follow-up lessons, as noted in the "Reasons for Revisiting This Text" discussed in depth in Chapter 8.

There Sure Are a Lot of Questions Here

There are indeed a lot of questions specified in this during-reading part of the lesson. "We're not going to ask **all** of these questions, are we?" teachers often want to know. You might not ask every one of *these* questions, but at the beginning of this close reading process, there will be a lot of questions, and you (the teacher) will be doing most of the asking. As time goes on, students will be doing much more of the questioning themselves, as we teach them to internalize these kinds of questions. We'll talk about that in our discussion in Chapter 7, Moving Students Toward Independence in Close Reading.

It just makes sense that if we want elementary-grade students to understand a text deeply, we will need to help guide them there. When the text is complex, there is a lot to discover about it—hence, so many questions. But maybe not these exact questions. I prefer not to distribute my lesson plan to teachers before I teach a close reading lesson to their students because I don't want them checking off the questions as I come to them. My lessons sometimes take a few unanticipated twists and turns because I follow the children. Their response to an initial question may set up a follow-up question that I didn't consider when I first wrote my plan. Remember, though, that "following the children" means into the text, not into the vagaries of their personal connections.

A final critical point to make about the during-reading part of a close reading lesson is that analyzing the text is not synonymous with having a "discussion" about the text. True, many of the questions included in this lesson are higher level and divergent. There will certainly be varying responses, and that is fine as long as students base their responses on evidence that comes from the text. Keep in mind, however, that your main goal in the initial close reading of any text is to uncover the *author's* meaning. This will keep your lesson on track. Once the author's meaning has been discerned, returning to specific points in the text for an academic discussion is a great focus for a follow-up lesson (and helps you meet Common Core criteria for the Listening and Speaking Standards, too.)

Now that you've had this up-close view of what happens in the during-reading part of your close reading lesson, take some time to reflect on the following questions—with your professional learning community, a colleague, or on your own—before moving forward to the next chapter on supporting readers *after* close reading.

Reflecting on What We Know

1. The way we approach a text during close reading is complicated by our need to be familiar with the College and Career Readiness Anchor Standards for Reading. What do you understand clearly about these standards now? What do you need to spend more time learning about?

2. Even though our state and district standards in the past have addressed many of the same literary terms and elements addressed by the Common Core (vocabulary, theme, connections, etc.), it would be fair to say that the Common Core's approach is quite different in some cases. What important differences do you see in this new approach to reading comprehension? Which standards do you regard as the most challenging—for you and for your students? Why?

3. To what extent are your current questions for the texts you teach "text dependent"? Reflect (honestly) on some of the questions that have accompanied texts you've read with your students. What questions might you eliminate based on this need for text dependence?

4. Look at the charts Close Reading Questions Aligned to Common Core's College and Career Readiness Anchor Standards for Reading (Figure 5.2) on page 86 and Recognizing the Author's Craft During Close Reading (Figure 5.3) on page 90. Which questions that you may not be asking now might be good additions to your close reading instruction?

5. Look one more time at the text-dependent questions for "She Was *THAT* Kind of Lady." Try to think of additional questions that are well matched to this text. Can you identify the standard aligned to each of your new questions?

6. Using the same text you used in Chapters 2, 3, and 4, now plan just the during-reading part of your lesson using the blank Planning for Close Reading template found in Appendix I and on the book's companion website at **www.corwin.com/closerreading**.

7. What was hard about doing this part of your lesson plan? What was easy? What questions do you have about designing this part of your lesson? If possible, share and discuss your work here with another colleague or colleagues who are also working on close reading.

Supporting Readers *After* Close Reading

Instructional Shift

Before the Common Core	With the Common Core
Scaffolding after reading: After reading, students were typically tasked with writing a response to a question that aligned with a discrete lesson objective: What is the theme? What trait did the character demonstrate? And so on.	**Scaffolding after reading:** After close reading, students are tasked with producing both oral and written responses, synthesizing and integrating information from multiple print and nonprint sources.

The Instructional Shift

When I saw some early versions of sample assessment items from Smarter Balanced Assessment Consortium (SBAC), I noticed that many of the performance tasks included opportunities for oral response as a component of the assessment process. These were not among the parts of the task to be scored. The purpose was simply to give students time to talk through some of the reading they had done in small collaborative groups before they responded individually to written questions. This honored not only the importance of oral response (technically "oral rehearsal") as a precursor to written response but also the value of peer collaboration. I was elated!

There is a great deal of support for the significance of "oral rehearsal" before written response, especially for students who struggle with language (including English learners): "It is axiomatic that if students do not have the ability to express their ideas orally, they will not be able to express their ideas in writing. Oral language and written language are inextricably linked" (Williams, Stathis, & Gotsch, 2008, p. 2). Similarly, there is evidence that ideas generated in interactive conversations during reading instruction often reappear later in students' writing (Fitzgerald & Amendum, 2007).

Unfortunately, the more recently posted sample assessment tasks—for either of the assessment consortia (SBAC or PARCC, Partnership for Assessment of Readiness for College and Careers)—generally omit mention of opportunities for oral rehearsal, except when the student proficiency to be assessed is a target in the Listening and Speaking standards. So while I can say that the Common Core appears to support a shift toward oral response preceding written response, I cannot legitimately say that the *assessments* support that.

What I can say with assurance, however, is that the Common Core assessments demonstrate a shift toward measuring students' capacity to integrate and synthesize information from multiple sources. And this is here to stay. If students are to succeed with these more rigorous assessments, we need to make some significant changes to the after-reading support we provide. And one change should be more systematic attention to oral collaboration.

Recognizing the Error of Our Ways

Over the last decade or so, teachers have felt compelled to move to written response after reading, with barely a breath between the last paragraph of the text and the written task that followed. This had a lot to do with high-stakes assessments that relied heavily on similar types of questions. *Practice makes perfect,* reasoned teachers, and so students practiced and practiced and practiced—until after a while, they just didn't care anymore. Responding to text became more of a rote exercise than an impassioned reflection. No wonder we ended up with some pretty mediocre scores.

In many cases, there hasn't been after-reading *support*; there has only been after-reading *assessment.* Students read their assigned text with an eye to the specific objective guiding the day's lesson; then the teacher posted a question aligned with this objective, and students wrote their response. The scaffolding that was present guided the written response, perhaps in the form of an answer organizer or an answer frame, but it did not guide students' reflection about what they read.

In many cases there hasn't been after-reading support; there has only been after-reading assessment.

I have no issue with answer frames and organizers. In fact, I wrote two books that can be very helpful in teaching students how to produce well-organized and elaborated answers to open-ended questions—*Teaching Written Response to Text* and *That's a GREAT Answer!* (see Boyles, 2001 and 2011, respectively). There is a place for these supports, but they should not (and never were intended to) replace what we do to help students get ready to respond.

We must rethink what students really need between the time they finish their close reading text and the time they pick up their pencils to write their responses to an assessment question. What can we do to help them get ready to respond? We can routinely provide them with a repertoire of *tasks* that will reinforce their comprehension. And we can make sure that the *process* through which they engage in these tasks is as productive as possible.

Consider the After-Reading Process

If we want students to become confident, articulate comprehenders, we need to let them talk about what they read. *Talking about* their reading, I must point out, is different from *discussing* their reading as we typically define a book discussion—with teachers asking questions and students responding or students asking each other questions. Of course, there is a place for thoughtful discussion of a text, and much of this will happen *during* close reading, as described in the previous chapter of this book. A rousing discussion *after* reading can also enhance understanding. But what I have in mind here isn't really about questions and answers.

"Talking it out" is aimed at getting students to invest more of themselves in the response process.

How can we get kids to care, to "own" the process? The missing piece of this puzzle, in my view, is collaborative oral response—for two reasons. First, as I remind teachers over and over, if students can't *say* it, it's doubtful they will be able to *write* it. This will be even truer with the types of tasks students will be expected to accomplish to meet the goals of the Common Core. Many questions in the assessments are complex, involving multiple texts and integration of knowledge that represents so much more than a one-to-one correspondence between a discrete objective and a test item.

Giving students the opportunity to "talk it out" with a partner or small group of peers—no matter what "it" is—before answering assessment questions on paper also yields more motivation and buy-in. As students explore some aspect of a text together, they will become more personally invested, determining their own point of view and verbally defending their claims. They will also get to listen to the way others form thoughts into sentences with an opportunity to model the language of their responses after the sentences they've heard from other group members. "Oral rehearsal" preceding written response will provide many students with the courage they need to ultimately "publish" their thinking on paper. This is especially critical for English language learners short on both the competence and confidence to articulate their thinking on paper.

Talking about *reading is different from* discussing *their reading as we typically define a book discussion—with teachers asking a series of questions and students responding.*

If students can't say it, it's doubtful they will be able to write it.

But just telling students to "turn and talk" or "get into small groups" will not automatically accomplish this goal. I am in a lot of classrooms, and I can tell right away when this small-group or partner activity is going to flourish or when it is going to fall flat. In not-so-successful situations, the teacher announces even a simple turn-and-talk activity, and chaos ensues. The popular kids clamber over each other to get to their best buddy, leaving other students "partnerless" (the very ones for whom this interaction is most critical). In the worst scenarios, I've seen students go so far as to refuse to work with a classmate if the teacher assigns the matches: *I'm not working with HIM!*

There are other classrooms, though, where students engage with classmates with respect and compassion. In these best-case scenarios, the teacher has built a culture of collaboration. Children can learn to be inclusive rather than exclusive. They can practice the language they will need to welcome a child without a partner into their group. They can learn how to listen to their peers and how to take the lead when it is their turn. They can learn how to be accountable to themselves and their group. But we have to teach them *how*. With this process firmly in place, the outcomes of the process—the tasks we ask students to complete—will more accurately measure their literacy competence.

Develop a Strong Repertoire of After-Reading Tasks

With close reading, the after-reading *tasks* we provide to our students will be more important than ever. During reading, we have painstakingly pulled the text apart line by line, word by word. Now we need to put it all back together so students can appreciate the big picture. I suggest a repertoire of tasks, some of which will apply to *all* texts, and others that you will want to select judiciously for their application to *particular* texts.

First, there are four essential after-reading tasks (described in the next section) that you will *always* want students to complete. Keep the following points in mind as you incorporate them after close reading:

- Sometimes these tasks may be accomplished on the same day you read your text, if time allows and the text is especially short. Most frequently, however, lack of sufficient time will mean you will return to these points the next day as a culmination of your lesson.

- Sometimes these tasks may be completed quickly, rapid fire "mentions" that regularly follow close reading once students have learned how to handle them. At other times, depending on students' preparation and the process through which they complete them, the tasks may take several minutes.

- Sometimes we will want students to complete these tasks in response to texts they read independently in addition to their shared, close reading texts. Consistency is key if we want these reading tasks to become reading habits.

The Four Essential Follow-Up Tasks

Task 1: Identify the Key Words— Both in and *About* the Text

Earlier in this book, I made the point that *collecting important words* during reading is critical to comprehension. After reading, the very first thing readers should do is take stock of those words:

- What are they?
- Why are they important?
- Did I miss any "good ones" along the way?

When you think about it, it's virtually impossible to talk about reading without these key words: the people or characters, places, items, and so forth that are mentioned over and over again. But there's another, more subtle kind of word that students should also be able to identify: What are the key words *about* the text that may not actually be *in* the text? These words often have to do with values, underlying problems, or emergent themes.

For example, I share numerous books and documents with students that are related to the civil rights era. Words like *discrimination, prejudice, segregation,* and *integration* are not actually in these texts. But they capture the big ideas, and students will be able to talk about the text more efficiently if they have command over them. They should come up *during* reading. But students should also return to them *after* reading. When they talk and write about the text, we will want to hear *both* kinds of words in the language they use.

Identifying the important words can be done quickly after reading as a whole-class follow-up or in partnerships or small groups as a collaborative task. For the small-group task, you might want to use the organizer Most Important Words (Template 1). This is a good resource to use for students to "talk it out," as their conversation with peers will help them clarify not only word meanings but also which words really are the most important. I typically tell students how many words they can choose. I want them to be selective, not listing every possible word, but a few words that are most central to the text's meaning.

Although classroom-ready materials for other chapters are provided within the chapter each supports, the Most Important Words organizer and all other templates for after-reading tasks have been placed in Appendix III at the end of this book. With so many templates included (fourteen in all), they will be easier to access in their very own space where you can more easily examine them together. The templates may also be found on the book's companion website at **www.corwin.com/closerreading.**

Task 2: Identify the Key Idea (Theme/Lesson/Message/Main Idea)

Identifying the theme or main idea is something else students should always practice when they have finished reading; this will be especially important with the complex texts we use for close reading. Teachers speak to me all the time about how difficult it is for their students to figure out theme. I think some of this is because we try to teach it as a "skill." It's the "skill of the week" or the unit or maybe even just a particular lesson. Then we move on to another unit with another skill, and *theme* is no longer at the top of our agenda. I think we'd do better to think of uncovering theme as the natural outgrowth of any text we read. We can talk about what the story is "starting to be about" right from the beginning of the text. But we should *always* circle back to this point at the end to clarify the message.

This brings up another complicating issue: There are so many labels that seem to be used synonymously here: theme, message, lesson, big idea. How do we handle this? I personally like the notion of "author's message" because even fairly young children know what a "message" is. I think this term captures the intent of what we're hoping students will uncover. But we also can't neglect "proper" terminology like *theme*. We know that to meet the Common Core Standards, academic vocabulary is critical. And repeatedly hearing a word like *theme* prepares students for the academic language they will encounter in higher grades and on assessments. One distinction I make for students is between *lesson* and *theme*. I tell them this:

The *lesson* in the story is what the *character* learns.

The *theme* is what we learn as readers.

Although this is a bit of an oversimplification, it works quite well. Another distinction students need to understand is between *topic* and *theme* or *main idea*. This is how I explain it:

The *topic* is often a single word—like *friendship* or *penguins*.

Theme or main idea is something *about* the topic. For example:

○ *Loyalty is important to a friendship.*

○ *Climate change threatens penguins.*

Main idea is typically a term applied to informational works and generally relates to a short text or part of a longer text, not a whole book on some informational topic. In fact, most longer informational works do not have just one *main idea*. Different parts of the text are organized around different central points. This is the way the Common Core approaches main idea, as well.

Informational texts do not really have *themes*. Rather, different authors focus on an aspect of a topic differently. For example, one author may focus on Abraham Lincoln's childhood and his love of books (*Abe Lincoln: The Boy Who Loved Books* by Kay Winters), while another may emphasize Lincoln's legacy and the nuances of his personal life (*Looking at Lincoln* by Maira Kalman).

Do literary texts have *main ideas*? I often ask students to identify the main idea of a paragraph or even a chapter in a piece of fiction. But we don't find the *theme* of a paragraph or short portion of a text. *Theme* is reserved for the central message of the literary work as a whole. Of course, many texts have multiple themes; we should not insist that our students find just one theme. And *their* theme can be different from the one *we* find—as long as they can justify it with textual evidence.

Identifying a theme (or themes) can be difficult for students because of the abstract thinking involved. We can make it easier by beginning with a preconstructed list of possible themes and asking children to select the one that's the best match for their current text. This is the premise on which the Theme Chart is built, a good starting point for regular, consistent work on theme.

Here's how the theme chart (Template 2) works:

- Determine four or five themes that recur in texts at your grade level. Included might be such big ideas as these:

  o *Discrimination hurts.*

  o *Hard work helps you achieve your dreams.*

  o *Friends support us in different ways.*

- List these themes down the left-hand column of the chart. You will want to make sure that the first few texts you read are a match for the themes you've listed.

- As students identify them through their close reading, write the title of a book or place an image of the cover in the cell next to that theme. Soon you will have several texts specified for each theme—perfect for text-to-text connections.

There will also come a time (not too far into this process) when students come to the end of a reading selection and tell you, "I don't think any of the themes on our chart go with this book." This is a good sign that this notion of theme is really catching on and that your students are ready to determine themes more independently. Add new themes as students discover them themselves.

Task 3: Create a Summary or Gist Statement

If students know the key words in a text and can recognize its theme, providing a brief summary or gist statement is a fairly straightforward next step. Begin with the theme. Then ask students to think about what the author did to *show* that theme. I like the idea of asking for a gist statement because it's short and sweet, about twenty words that highlight what's *most* important to remember about a text. For example, for an article about mammoths, a suitable gist statement might be this:

> *A mammoth's body was well suited to the cold and helped protect it from the harsh weather during the Ice Age.*

Notice that there are no details here, only the main point of the piece with key words cited: (*mammoths* and *Ice Age*)

If it's something a little more detailed that you want, go with a summary. I ask students for a four-sentence summary. Tell me the theme or main idea, followed by three sentences with supporting information. For the mammoth piece: *A wooly mammoth's body helped it survive during the Ice Age. Its tusks scraped ice off grass. Its hump stored fat in case food couldn't be found. Its long, shaggy fur kept it warm.*

Both of these formats require students to put information into their own words, to paraphrase. There is a place in reader response for direct quotes, but not necessarily within gist statements and brief summaries. A template for a gist statement and two summary protocols is provided (Template 3) in case this support is needed. This also might be a good time for some peer collaboration. You would ask students to complete just one of the bottom sections, depending on what they are summarizing.

Task 4: Review the Text Structure and Genre

In Chapter 4, I discussed the importance of identifying the probable text type (literary or informational) *before* reading to guide students' comprehension. Even without a lot of knowledge about a text, from the cover alone students can generate a reasonable hypothesis in most cases about whether the text will be literary or informational: *Am I looking for story parts or facts?* But after reading, they have much more information and should be able to name not only the basic text type but also its *structure* and *genre*. Including this as part of the after-reading conversation affords an opportunity to expand students' recognition of structural elements and genre features. Unfortunately, many primary-grade teachers spend so little time introducing different text structures and genres that students arrive in the intermediate grades with little foundation on which to build.

Structure. If you are starting from scratch, you will want to begin with just a few basic text structures. For example:

- **Problem/solution.** Can students identify all of the story parts (characters, setting, problem, events, solution)?
- **Sequence of events.** Can students identify the steps in the process or the order through which events unfold?
- **Cause and effect.** Can students identify one or more instances of cause-and-effect in the reading?
- **Compare and contrast.** Can students identify two or more different points of view presented in the reading and explain the differences?
- **Descriptive.** Can students identify *who* or *what* is being described and how the author brings the description to life (imagery, figurative language, and other literary devices)?
- **Main idea and supporting details.** Can students identify the main idea and the details that support it?

Moreover, can students draw a simple diagram depicting each of these? A diagram can make a structure more visible.

Genre. After students have identified the structure, we can move on to genre: Is it a tall tale, a legend, an "all-about" book? What qualities did this text demonstrate that are similar to or different from other texts you have read: a fairy tale, a myth, a life cycle book? Making these kinds of text-to-text comparisons will solidify understanding of various genres, knowledge students can bring to the next text they read. It will also be useful for the next story or informational piece they *write*. Genre is a wonderful link for connecting reading and writing. But none of this will be possible if students lack a basic knowledge of the characteristics of different genres.

Bringing students up to speed with genre characteristics requires that teachers understand these characteristics, too. You can begin by making sure that you (and your students) know the difference between text *structure* and text *genre*. Think of it this way: There are just a few basic structures (see those identified above) that dominate most of the reading students do in school. But many genres fall within each genre. The chart Text Structures and Related Genres (Figure 6.1) will help clarify this structure-genre distinction.

For a deeper understanding of genres frequently encountered by students in the intermediate grades, see the second edition of my book, *That's a GREAT Answer! Teaching Literature Response Strategies to Elementary, ELL, and Struggling Readers* (Boyles, 2011). The CD in the back of this book contains a genre packet that you can download. The packet (in the file "Teaching About Genre") includes task sheets for thirteen genres, highlighting academic vocabulary students will need to talk about the genre. Each task sheet also presents a list of genre characteristics that students can look for and check off as they read. These, too, support oral collaboration among peers—and independence from direct teacher instruction.

If they already understand structure and genre, the conversation you have with your students after an initial close reading may be a brief, two-minute recap where they fire off all of the characteristics they've observed in the text. If their insights are more limited, that will alert you to the need for a follow-up text structure or genre lessons. The organizer Noticing Text Structure and Genre (Template 4) will support this focus *after* students have acquired some knowledge of genre characteristics.

Templates For "Talking It Out" After Reading

You will find fourteen after-reading tasks identified in Table 6.1, List of After-Reading Tasks. This list includes the four tasks described above as well as ten additional tasks that encourage students to dig even deeper into individual texts. Remember that it's not just the *task* that is important but also the *process* through which the task is completed. That is why engaging in these tasks should always incorporate an opportunity for students to "talk it out." For each task, there is a brief statement of its purpose and how the purpose correlates with the Common Core College and Career Anchor Standards for Reading.

You may wonder why students need an organizer when they are just "talking it out." Keep in mind that templates provide structure for students' conversations and inspire a sense of accountability. Also remember that some students clarify their thinking as they write. If students make notes during their group discussions, they will also be better prepared for a follow-up whole-class share and for a written response if one is required later on.

While some of these may seem a bit advanced for students in the intermediate grades, they lead to the development of skills important to our ultimate goal: college

Figure 6.1

Text Structures and Related Genres

Text Structure	Related Genres
Problem/solution	• Realistic fiction • Fairy tales • Folk tales • Myths and legends • Historical fiction • Mysteries • Adventure stories • Fables
Sequence of events	• Some personal narratives • Biographies • Journal or "letter" texts • Chapters from a chapter book • "How-to" books • Life cycle books • Narrative nonfiction
Expository (Main idea/detail)	• "All-about" books • Essays • Most content area materials with headings/subheadings • Speeches
Compare/contrast	• Letters to the editor (two points of view) • Stories told from two or more perspectives
Cause/effect	• Advertisements • Social or scientific problems
Description	• Travel brochures • Some poetry • Introduction to some literary texts • Some personal narratives
News event (5 w/h): **Who, what, when, where, why, how**	• Newspaper articles • Interviews

 Available for download at **www.corwin.com/closerreading**

and career readiness. If we hold the bar high and provide students with the tools and support to get there, they will be able to succeed even when the challenge is great. When choosing which of these tasks to use, think about your text as well as your students:

- What *special features* does this text include that students would benefit from discussing?
- What *skills* need a bit more reinforcement and conversation?

Table 6.1

List of After-Reading Tasks

Template	Title	Description of Task	Standard
1	Most Important Words	Students identify words that are key to meaning—and explain *why* they are important.	Standard 4: Vocabulary
2	Theme Chart	Students identify themes that align with texts they have read on a matrix, setting up the opportunity for text-to-text connections by theme.	Standard 2: Theme
3	Gist Statement and Brief Summary	Students create brief summaries that include the theme or even shorter gist statements that exclude details.	Standard 2: Summary that includes theme
4	Noticing Text Structure and Genre	Students identify features of various text structures and genres and match them to their close reading text.	Standard 5: Text structure and genre
5	Evidence From First Close Reading of a Text	Students are asked to identify a range of findings from a close reading: important words, gist/summary, other observations.	All standards
6	Paraphrase It!	Students find a quote to support a statement about the text, then put it into their own words.	Standard 2: Paraphrase
7	Words That Show Tone	Students identify words that show *how* the author is creating tone through word use.	Standard 4: Vocabulary
8	Looking Into Illustrations	Students learn how to "read" an illustration—such as those in picture books.	Standard 7: Different kinds of texts

Template	Title	Description of Task	Standard
9	Viewing a Video	Students learn how to get content information from a video and recognize media features.	Standard 7: Different kinds of texts
10	Reading a Photograph	Students learn how to "read" a photograph as a source of information.	Standard 7: Different kinds of texts
11	Evaluating an Argument	Students learn various criteria for critiquing a source for validity and reliability.	Standard 8: Critiquing text Standard 6: Author's purpose
12	Reading and Evaluating a Primary Source	Students learn the questions they should consider when evaluating a primary source document.	Standard 8: Critiquing text
13	Reading Like a Scientist	Students learn the questions a scientist asks when reading and analyzing science information.	Standard 8: Critiquing text
14	Reading Like a Historian	Students learn the questions a historian asks when reading and analyzing information about history.	Standard 8: Critiquing text

A Note About Written Tasks

It is certainly acceptable and useful for students to respond in writing to a question related to their close reading text, and even for teachers to evaluate students' reading proficiency based on such responses. However, this should be viewed as an *extension* of the lesson or assessment rather than as a component of the lesson itself. One of the primary focuses of the Common Core is the *integration of knowledge,* and it will be important to incorporate writing tasks into your curriculum, though now this will often happen after reading and synthesizing more than a single text. This may mean fewer writing tasks after individual close reads.

When OUR AFTER-READING INSTRUCTION Goes Off Track

I am concerned about two things that could take our after-reading support off track.

1. The inclination to move too quickly to written response. Aside from leading to less than spectacular answers to those comprehension questions, another unfortunate outcome is that students draw the conclusion that the real reason they're doing this reading is so they can answer a test question. This is not the message we want to send. We want our approach to close reading to demonstrate that there is value in the reading itself. That is why we want to take the time after reading to engage with the text in thoughtful, even "playful" ways through collaboration and talk.

2. Making the after-reading component too "activity based," a random exercise with no clear connection to students' needs or the dictates of the text. The strength of the four primary after-reading tasks described above is the way we use them together, regularly and systematically, to help children make meaning and deepen their understanding. (Note that engaging in these tasks will not always involve the task sheets.) The value of the additional tasks is to help students delve deeper into aspects of particular texts that are significant for one reason or another. If we pull out one of these graphic organizers willy-nilly and "assign it" for students to complete as an after-reading exercise without benefit of collaboration with their peers, we will essentially be turning these tasks into a new millennium version of dittos. Let's not do that!

Applying What We Know

Completing the After-Reading Part of Our Close Reading Plan

Now that we've examined what should happen *after* reading to reinforce students' understanding of *any* text and the pitfalls we want to avoid, let's decide what we might do to solidify their comprehension of *this* text.

First, "She Was *THAT* Kind of Lady" is long enough that the after-reading part of the lesson would almost certainly occur the next day. With any tasks, a key consideration is which ones have already been modeled and practiced so that students can apply them independently and which ones need further guidance for ease of use. Let's assume this lesson will be taught early in the school year before students have had much experience with either close reading or with any of these after-reading tasks. How should we proceed? See the planner in Figure 6.2 (for a blank version, see Appendix I and the book's companion website at **www.corwin.com/closerreading**) for a quick view of what my plan with our hypothetical group of fourth graders might look like. Following the planner is an explanation of my thinking.

Figure 6.2

Planning For Close Reading

(Sample)

After Reading

(Depending on time available, some tasks below may not be completed on same day as first close reading)

Follow-up tasks for close reading:

1. Important words to talk about the text:

(whole class—quick oral response)

Words *in* the text: Gram, porch, old-fashioned, people, stories

Words *about* the text: generosity, kindness, admired

2. Theme/lesson/message:

(turn and talk with partner; whole-class share)
Theme about Gram:
- Happiness comes from the simple things in life and from giving to others;

Theme about the granddaughter:
- Sometimes the people we admire most aren't those who accomplish great deeds, but those who live their lives with kindness toward others.

3. Summary or gist statement:

(whole class—quick oral response)

Create a gist statement:

- A kind, generous grandmother who was happy with simple things in life was loved and admired by her family and friends.

4. Structure and genre:

(small-group collaborative activity; see "Talk it out" below)

Memoir: A collage of memories about someone special to the author, showing how the subject related to the time and place in which she lived, and the important people in her life

5. Optional: Additional task related to this text or students' skill needs:

Not included for this initial close reading

Talk it out:

Noticing Text Structure and Genre (complete template in small groups)

[Written task]

Not included for this initial close reading

Available for download at **www.corwin.com/closerreading**

Considerations for Close Reading Instruction: After Reading

Identify important words to talk about the text: I would begin the after-reading part of my lesson by addressing the "word" issue quickly with the whole class, charting words as students suggest them. I try to stay away from words related to details like *washing machine and clothesline,* etc., because once you start listing those, there is almost no end to the possibilities—and students don't need them for a gist statement, which is how they will use them here. I would also make sure that students could identify a few key words *about* the text since these will be crucial to explaining the theme. They would not have to mention the exact words indicated on the planner in Figure 6.2; any reasonable synonyms would be fine.

Identify the key idea (theme/lesson/message/main idea): As noted earlier, a deeper theme of this text—the author's perception of her grandmother—would need a follow-up lesson addressing point of view, with some attention to the words that revealed this point of view. But even after an initial close reading, students should be able to explain a theme related to Gram—that she was the kind of person who enjoyed the simple things in life and that it was her generosity and thoughtfulness that made her who she was. I would have students do a quick turn-and-talk to begin to articulate their thinking about this. Then we would share ideas aloud.

Create a summary or gist statement: This *could* be another turn-and-talk opportunity. But my goal is to get to the "talk it out" portion of the lesson. Hence, I would most likely segue quickly to developing a gist statement with the whole class, again charting it. Something like this: *A kind, generous grandmother who was happy with simple things in life was loved and admired by her family and friends.* Kids love counting the words to see if we can get close to the prescribed twenty.

Identify text structure and genre: Although students may not bring much prior knowledge to this part of the lesson, they would have enough understanding of the text to discover some of the genre characteristics on their own. For example, they could recognize that this memoir focuses heavily on someone the narrator knows very well. They might notice the setting is integral to the sequence of events. They might notice that there are other people who are important to the main character. This would be a good opportunity for some collaborative work with peers. See "talk it out" below for how this could be accomplished.

Talk it out: Assuming very little experience in determining genre and no previous work with memoir, I would first divide the class into small groups of three or four students each and then distribute copies of the organizer Noticing Text Structure and Genre. Although I could let groups think through the text structure on their own, this would likely add too many minutes to the activity, resulting in off-task behaviors. So we would think about the structure together. This would go pretty fast because they would be able to rule out most structures immediately: problem/solution, sequence, main idea/details, and so on. I would want them to recognize that this text is primarily *descriptive*, and I would probably draw a web with Gram's name in the middle, spokes leading to the various details that could be inserted (though I wouldn't take the time to add all these details).

Then we would move on to the task itself. Groups would be instructed to notice characteristics of the text. I would give them an example to get started: *You get lots of details about where Gram lived.* The sheet asks for three genre characteristics, and I think that's a reasonable number. Groups would be told they have seven minutes to get the job done. (Five minutes is too brief a time to accomplish much of anything; ten minutes leads to irrelevant side conversations; I've always found seven minutes to be just about right.) I would make sure before letting them get to work that each group had appointed a recorder and that they understood what they must have to show for their efforts at the end of our seven minutes: *Go!*

There's always an immediate buzz in the room during collaborative activities, and I scurry from group to group observing the action. Children thrive on these opportunities to "talk it out." I give a "one-minute warning" to finish recording their final thought, and when that time is up, each group shares. If a group hasn't identified all three criteria, no problem. Among all of us, we have lots of good ideas, and in the end, we name our genre. Although students may not have had much prior knowledge to bring to this task today, they will have more of it the next time they read a text with these characteristics.

Written task: There is no written task identified as a follow-up to this lesson as students are just beginning their study of memoir in general and of this text in particular.

Before moving on to the next chapter to learn more about moving students to independence with close reading, consider the following questions—with your professional learning community, a colleague, or on your own. You might also want to look at the whole lesson plan from start to finish. For that, see Appendix II. Since we created this plan step-by-step, examining the way its parts fit together will give you a better sense of its flow.

Reflecting on What We Know

1. In your school/district/state, has there been a strong emphasis on written response? What outcomes have resulted—both positive and negative?

2. Think about the four essential after-reading tasks discussed in this chapter. Do they seem useful to you the way they are described here as a regular repertoire of points to be clarified after close reading? Explain why or why not.

3. Are there any other tasks or questions you would also want to emphasize after reading? What are they? Why are they important to emphasize?

4. Survey the task templates included in this chapter. Which ones would you like to try with your students? Why? How could they help achieve your close reading goals and the goals of the Common Core Standards?

5. Using the same text you used in previous chapters, now plan the after-reading part of your lesson using the blank Planning for Close Reading template with work spaces, located in Appendix I or available at **www.corwin.com/closerreading**. What was hard about doing this? What was easy? What questions do you have about designing this part of your lesson? If possible, share and discuss your work here with another colleague who is also working on close reading.

6. You have now finished designing your complete lesson for before, during, and after close reading. Have a go at teaching it. Reflect on the outcome with a colleague or your professional learning community. Share ideas:

   - What went well?
   - What didn't go so well?
   - Why did it go this way?
   - What will you do differently next time?
   - How might you proceed with your instruction on a subsequent day in order to dig deeper into this text?

CHAPTER 7

Moving Students Toward Independence in Close Reading

Instructional Shift

Before the Common Core	With the Common Core
Moving students toward independence: The goal of reading instruction has always been to move students to independence, but lately it has been more focused on independence with an *objective*.	**Moving students toward independence:** We need to help students become more independent in retrieving all of the meaning from a text *themselves*—without a teacher by their side to guide them.

The Instructional Shift

When I was first introduced to the concept of close reading instruction as a means of helping students achieve the goals of the Common Core, I wasn't sure I liked this idea one bit. Actually, I liked the idea of close reading just fine, especially the move toward appreciation of the whole text rather than just the evidence in support of an isolated objective. What distressed me were the implications for *instruction*, the way close reading would be delivered to students via teacher-directed *text-dependent questions* day after day after day.

Where's the gradual release? I wanted to know. I have long been an advocate of explicit instruction, that practice of initiating a lesson with a clear explanation, modeling as needed, then providing diminishing levels of guided support until students could manage on their own. The best teaching leads to transfer, applying a concept learned today to tomorrow's text a little more competently and independently than it was applied today. I saw the potential for none of this with close reading the way it was initially described to me: How could a bunch of text-dependent questions about the moons of Jupiter inform tomorrow's reading on Duke Ellington? I pondered this problem for a while—during which time I made a couple of useful discoveries.

My first aha moment came about because I gave text-dependent questions a chance. What I began to see as I returned to the same classrooms to teach multiple close reading lessons was that students used the questions *I* asked as models for the types of insights they could seek *themselves* within other texts. For example, after reading the poem "Autumn" (Emily Dickinson), some third graders eagerly pointed out personification when we came to it in Cynthia Rylant's picture book, *In November*— no prompting whatsoever. Students in other classes reading other texts showed this same capacity for transfer. We sometimes forget the power of teaching by example— and what better example could there be for literacy instruction than rich questions that teach readers how to examine a text closely? This notion of rich questions led me to my second source of independence.

If students were able to model their thinking about a text after mine, maybe I could teach them a few basic queries to always ask themselves during close reading. They would need to be general questions, the kind that could work for any text. I came up with four questions:

- What is the author telling me?
- What are the hard or important words?
- What does the author want me to understand?
- How does the author play with language to add to meaning?

Getting to Independence With Four Powerful Questions

1. What Is the Author Telling Me?

I reasoned that this first question would elicit literal thinking, helping students to monitor for meaning on their own. When you look at the kinds of during-reading questions I included on my lesson plan in Chapter 5, the initial question for each chunk of text frequently asked this same thing. Now my goal was to get students to ask themselves this question as well. Could they at least recognize the information the author was supplying in a particular part of the text? Could they put that

We sometimes forget the power of teaching by example—and what better example could there be for literacy instruction than rich questions that teach readers how to examine a text closely?

meaning into their own words? Asking this question would always be a good place to begin to check basic understanding.

2. Are There Any Hard or Important Words?

With repeated exposure to determining which words in a chunk of text are the most important, students become savvier about which words to designate as "important" when they're reading closely on their own. Even an awareness of words they don't understand that *might* be important will be helpful; those words can be investigated more fully at another time.

3. What Does the Author Want Me to Understand?

This question raises the bar a bit, moving from literal to inferential thinking: *What is the author showing instead of telling? What are the big ideas that you discover by reading between the lines?* As we ask pointed questions about underlying problems, personal motivations, and developing themes and main ideas, students will gain more insight into the potential of this question to unlock deeper meaning.

4. How Does the Author Play With Language to Add to Meaning?

This gets at all the author's craft we would like students to recognize. To work productively with this question, students need lots of exposure to the range of crafts noted for Standards 4 through 6 so they will know what a page of print can offer in this regard. Of all the questions, this is the one that will take the most practice for students to use independently. For your convenience, you will find these four powerful questions in various places in this book and on the reproducible templates provided. One place you will find them is on the poster in Figure 7.1.

I like the icon with the little detective, magnifying glass in hand, signifying that the job of the reader is to search for evidence. Some teachers have enlarged this poster and prominently displayed it on a bulletin board. As for me, I usually take my smaller, more portable version printed on 8½ × 11 card stock into classrooms and balance it on a ledge somewhere. I like to be able to draw students' attention to it as we pause at the end of each chunk of text. Each general question students can ask and answer for themselves is one less specific question I have to ask—and one step closer to independence. Over time, you should notice that you need to ask fewer and fewer directed questions. Indeed, we can move students toward independence in close reading, first through text-dependent questions and eventually by backing away from these questions.

Each general question students can ask and answer for themselves is one step closer to independence.

To remind you to work toward student independence right from the start in close reading instruction, you will find these questions on the lesson planning template under During Reading (see Appendix I and the book's companion website at **www.corwin.com/closerreading**). These questions are listed at the top and should precede the more directed questions specified for each chunk. Try to ask these four more general questions *first*; if your students struggle or their answers fail to demonstrate the depth of thinking you are seeking, move on to the more specific questions. These specific questions should really be more of a "backup plan."

Figure 7.1

What is the author telling me?
Any hard or important words?

What does the author want me to understand?

How does the author play with language to add to meaning?

 Available for download at **www.corwin.com/closerreading**

The truth is that when you first introduce close reading, you will need these backup questions most of the time. Students will not have had enough exposure to the fine points of text analysis to recognize the nuances of a text without prompting. Little by little, however, you should notice that students rely more on their own thinking and less on yours as they pursue meaning.

The final place you will find these questions is on the bookmark in Figure 7.2. Remember that close reading isn't just for whole-class lessons; it is also for work in small groups and especially in students' independent reading. More explanation of close independent reading can be found in the next chapter.

For even more information on close, independent reading, explore the work of other authors who also provide insight into this topic. Kylene Beers and Robert Probst (2013), in their book *Notice & Note: Strategies for Close Reading*, outline six "signposts" that students should "notice and note" as they come to them in text to promote deep comprehension: contrasts and contradictions, aha moment, tough questions, words of the wiser, again and again, and memory moment. Intended for upper-elementary, middle, and high school students, these strategies may be an appropriate next step for students who have learned to navigate the four more rudimentary questions I suggest.

Becoming a Strategic Independent Reader

There's more to becoming an independent close reader, however, than knowing which questions to ask yourself as you read. Students also need to know how to approach a text without their teacher always leading the way. This is where strategies for independence come into play. I'm not speaking of metacognitive strategies like visualizing and inferring (though those are handy to have around, too, as noted in Chapter 3). What I'm referring to here are the strategic behaviors that make us good readers—even if we don't consciously think about them. These are the things we need to teach our students how to do so that they can become strong independent readers, too.

I hadn't thought much about this until I started noticing a pattern emerging as I taught my close reading lessons. I found that my lessons were almost always taking longer than intended because I had to stop repeatedly and ask guiding questions to help students locate evidence and retrieve the evidence itself. It occurred to me that if we alerted students to some of these points to consider up front in a "launching unit" *before* attempting close reading, it would go a long way toward making them more independent. Our close reading lessons would then proceed more smoothly as well.

What good reader behaviors would *you* include in a close reading launching unit? What do you think we need to teach students *how to do* to become strong, independent readers? I asked a team of third-grade teachers recently. They suggested that students need to know what to do when their work is finished, where to put completed assignments, how to choose a book from the classroom library. They had a very long list when they were finished. Yes, these are the routines we typically

Little by little, you should notice that students rely more on their own thinking and less on yours as they pursue meaning.

Figure 7.2

Bookmark For Independent Close Reading

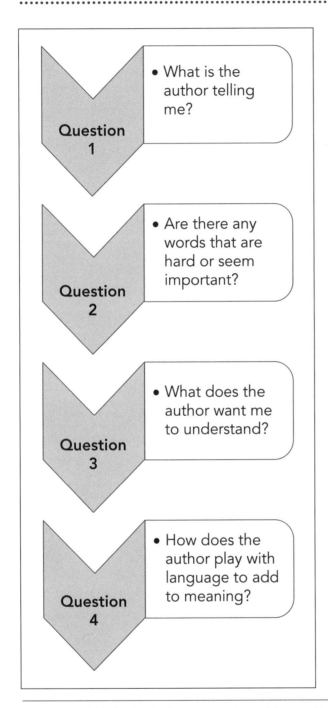

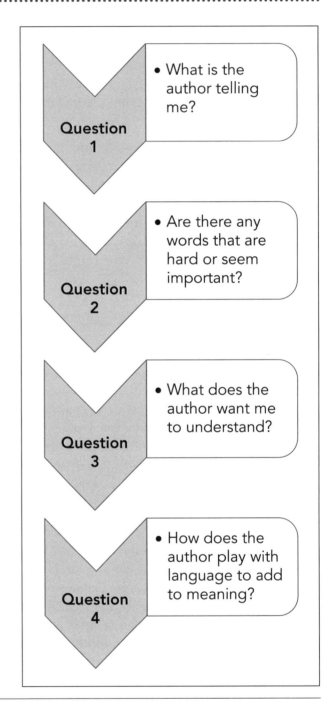

teach at the beginning of the school year, and they are indeed important to our mutual mental health. But they are not routines or considerations that will help students thrive as *independent close readers*. Let's think about the processes critical to close reading itself.

Minilessons for Independent Close Reading

If we think about what our students should know how to do as they approach a text, engage with a text, and reflect on a text in order to understand it deeply, we will have a pretty reliable list of processes we want them to internalize. My list is in Figure 7.3. I consider it a work in progress; I add new skills as I recognize other areas of student need.

Of course it's unlikely we'll be able to teach students to internalize these considerations for independent close reading so well that they will apply them automatically to every text. But teaching and then reinforcing how to do these things and encouraging students to make conscious decisions to practice them independently does gradually lead to more independence.

Strategy Minilessons

Although close reading can't be accomplished in a "minilesson," these lessons about how to approach, engage with, and reflect on a text are intended to be short—ten to fifteen minutes. A sample minilesson, Noticing Clues on the Cover, is provided in Figure 7.4. For this lesson, as with any lesson, it's just a matter of thinking about the way *you* approach some aspect of reading (in this case, looking at the cover) and then making that process visible to your students.

When you teach a minilesson for independent close reading, be clear about your purpose and make sure it's something specific. The focus should be one small component of learning to be an effective reader. You will see that I then identified several strategic points I wanted to be sure to share. There is no prescribed list of points to include for a lesson of this kind; any tidbit of information useful in your own reading will enhance students' strategic thinking.

It's also helpful when preparing for this type of minilessons to add the following:

- A few thoughts about what to look for when choosing a text to illustrate the strategy
- Some possible titles that would meet this need
- A follow-up task so students can practice their new learning

See the blank Minilesson Planning Template (Figure 7.5) to use as you design minilessons for independent close reading to meet the needs of *your* students.

Figure 7.3

Minilessons for Creating Reader Independence

What We Need to Teach Students How to Do

Before Reading: Approaching a Text

- Notice clues on the cover
- Notice clues in the layout of the pages
- Decide where to pause and think
- Decide how I will track my thinking and monitor my understanding
- Determine whether this text is literary or informational and decide what to look for in each type of text

During Reading: Engaging With a Text

- Think about what to look for on the first page
- Decide how to identify the narrator—and what the narrator cares about
- Identify the best evidence when reading literary text
- Identify the best evidence when reading informational text
- Decide what to do when I come to a word I can't pronounce or don't understand
- Use the four "good reader questions" that lead to understanding
- *Paraphrase* to show that understanding
- Look for author's craft in order to "read like a writer"
- Decide when it's helpful to use a particular comprehension strategy
- Decide what to do when I stop understanding
- Determine how the pictures or graphics in the text add to meaning
- Identify the most important words for talking about the text

After Reading: Reflecting on a Text

- Work well in a small group to respond to close reading
- Work well with a "turn-and-talk" partner to respond to close reading
- Know what to think about *after* reading to check understanding (four essential after-reading tasks: important words; author's message; summary; genre)
- Know how to create a *gist* statement to show understanding of the big idea
- Know what to include in a summary and what to leave out
- Know how to reflect on a text
- Know how to read a comprehension question to understand what it is asking
- Understand the academic language in assessment questions

Figure 7.4

Sample Minilesson For Independent Close Reading

Noticing Clues on the Cover

Purpose of this lesson: To help students develop a purpose for reading a particular text by noticing information on the cover, including title, author, and illustration; the purpose of this is <u>not</u> to spend a lot of time relating what's on the cover to background knowledge and personal connections.

Points to include in this lesson:

- Notice the title: What are the important words? Any hints about what the text will probably be about? Any words I don't understand that I will need to pay attention to as I read?

- Notice any illustrations: What people or objects are included that I will want to think about as I read? Does the size or placement of objects tell me anything about what might be important in the text?

- Notice the author: Is it an author I know? If so, what other books has the author written? What do I expect from this author?

- Information on the back cover: Is there helpful information on the back cover that gives me extra clues?

- Other: Is there a medallion on the cover that indicates the book received an award? What award? What does that tell me about the book?

- Literary or informational: Based on all the clues, do I think this book will be literary or informational?

When choosing a book to teach this lesson, look for the following: A book where the kinds of cover information (above) are helpful—or not helpful—to show that sometimes readers get really good information about the text from the cover and sometimes the information provided is *not* helpful.

Good books to use for a lesson about cover clues: *Those Shoes* by Maribeth Boelts; *More Than Anything Else* by Marie Bradby; *The Summer My Father Was Ten* by Pat Brisson; *Weslandia* by Paul Fleischman; *Four Feet Two Sandals* by Karen Lynn Williams

Follow-up task for independent reading: Independently, with a partner, or in small groups, have students choose a book and decide what they notice about it from the cover. What is the author/illustrator telling you—and what do you think the author/illustrator wants you to notice to get yourself ready to read? Share what you noticed with the whole class.

Figure 7.5

Minilesson Planning Template

Lesson Focus

Purpose of this lesson:

Points to include in this lesson:

When choosing a book to teach this lesson, look for the following:

Good books to use for a lesson about _____:

Follow-up task for independent reading: Independently, with a partner, or in small groups, have students . . .

When GETTING TO INDEPENDENCE Goes OFF Track

Two potential pitfalls concern me regarding this part of our instruction:

1. That teachers will take the emphasis on text-dependent questions to mean that the goal of our instruction is to help students get good at answering questions rather than to get good at reading closely and independently. We are bombarded with new initiatives in our classrooms. Not only do they compete for top billing on our list of instructional priorities, sometimes they actually seem to conflict with each other. "Are we still supposed to be doing that?" teachers inquire, recognizing that this strategy (or whatever) was the focus of professional development *last* year.

We need to acknowledge that moving students toward independence is not an "initiative," a fad that will vanish as rapidly as it appeared. Moving students toward independence should be the reason we get up in the morning, caffeinate ourselves, and head off to that big red schoolhouse.

2. That we will neglect to remove the scaffolds when children are ready for more independence. When we begin a lesson as I did for our close reading memoir text—Look at the cover . . . What important words do you see in the title . . . What details stand out in the cover illustration?—we are pleased that we have approached our text in a manner consistent with high-quality close reading instruction. And with good reason. This is what our teaching should look like when close reading is new to our students. But a month later—or even a couple of weeks later—there should be evidence that students are taking on more responsibility for learning themselves. This is where teachers sometimes go off track.

I see this too frequently. I visit a classroom to get teachers (and their students) started with close reading. The teachers observe carefully, and we have a productive conversation afterward, discussing details that will help them move forward with planning and teaching close reading themselves. Then I return in a month or so to see how close reading is going—and what I see is a mirror image of what I taught several weeks earlier. I'm sure these teachers think this will make me incredibly happy. However, I would be happier if I could see that students, even without prompting, were starting to ask their own "good reader" questions and activate their own strategies.

I now tell teachers, "When I come back in a month, I don't want to see the *next* lesson, I want to see a month's worth of progress. That means moving away from teacher dependence toward student independence." Not only do we need to set this as a goal, we need to take intentional steps to get there. Otherwise, our students will continue to look to us for every close reading move—which will not bode well for college and career readiness.

We can further strengthen students' independence in close reading, as well as the impact of close reading itself, by looking *beyond* the close reading lesson. Chapter 8 discusses what we can do to *extend* close reading, leading to even more independence. But before moving to that, take some time to reflect—in your professional learning community, with a colleague, or on your own—on the following questions.

Reflecting on What We Know

1. As teachers, we tend to provide students with the same level of support day after day, thinking that more practice will somehow lead to more independence. Most of the time, this doesn't really work. Think of something you have taught in the area of reading recently where you have moved students toward independence by gradually reducing the amount of support you provided. Explain how you did this step-by-step and share it with your group.

2. How might you use the four questions specified on the poster and bookmark to begin to move your students toward independence in close reading? Discuss.

3. Review the list of considerations for student independence before, during, and after close reading identified on page 124 (Figure 7.3). Are there any points you would add to this list? Which two or three of these points to consider would be especially helpful to your students? Why?

4. Using the Minilesson Planning Template on page 126 (Figure 7.5), design a minilesson for one of the points on the list or another point useful to your students. Teach your lesson. How did it go?

CHAPTER 8

Digging Deeper in Close Reading Through Rereading, Small-Group Instruction, and Independent Reading

Instructional Shift

Before the Common Core	With the Common Core
Digging deeper in close reading: There was little rereading or use of the text for other purposes because it had already served its purpose in supporting the objective; students moved on to a different text to apply the same objective.	**Digging deeper in close reading:** Rereading the entire text or portions of it is critical to even deeper comprehension. This is where focus and skill building should now occur; small-group instruction and independent reading should support close reading as well.

The Instructional Shift

Over the past several years, we've often operated under a "one-and-done" system of literacy instruction where students read a text one time to extract from it the evidence needed to support the day's objective. When that mission was complete, it was on to the next text to practice the same skill—hopefully with more proficiency and independence. This worked pretty well for building the desired skills. But as the Common Core has reminded us, it didn't do much over the long haul to enhance students' capacity to navigate complex text.

With close reading, the goal is to get better at understanding the text itself, so rereading becomes an essential part of the equation. We can reread for greater depth. We can also add breadth by connecting our close reading anchor text to standards beyond comprehension and to other texts. Finally, we need to recognize that students will not develop the close reading competence they need from shared reading alone. We need to add small-group instruction and independent reading to maximize its potential.

Planning to Revisit a Text

With close reading, the goal is to get better at understanding the text itself, so rereading becomes an essential part of the equation.

As I mentioned in Chapter 5, some close reading enthusiasts suggest that close rereading should involve reading through the entire text three times—each time noticing details that may have eluded students during an earlier reading. There will be times when rereading the whole text is very useful, depending on our *purpose.* For instance, if we want students to notice story events in order so they can write a sequential summary, it makes perfect sense to read the whole text again, from start to finish.

But taking this approach regularly may lead to a hefty chorus of groans from students short on patience for the task of rereading with no grander purpose than hoping to uncover a few new nuggets of literary knowledge. No, I don't think this will do much to increase anyone's appreciation for close reading! I believe that a better plan is to recognize what students did not uncover initially and focus more intently the second (or third) time around on the skills that would have provided a better grasp of those tricky parts of the text. Maybe students need a better sense of exactly how an author develops a theme. Maybe the main character's point of view would be more apparent if students recognized how the same story, told from *another* character's perspective, would be very different. Maybe students need help identifying words that contribute to tone.

After I've modeled a close reading lesson in someone's classroom, that teacher and usually others who also came to watch meet with me to talk about what they've observed and to discuss next steps. Almost always, the first question I get is, "So what would you do tomorrow now that you've finished this book?" Initially I was taken aback by this query, anticipating that instead teachers would be bursting with their own ideas for moving learning forward. I still believe that teachers *do* have lots of wonderful thoughts about appropriate follow-up, but they somehow imagine that my ideas will be better. Now, before answering I return the question to them: "What would *you* do?" We brainstorm together, excitement mounting, identifying an extensive range of options. Trust your instincts, teachers! You know your kids (and your texts) well and will make good choices.

The list of possible focus points for follow-up close reading lessons is practically endless. Keep in mind that the skills we develop don't all need to come from the Common Core Reading Standards. They can also support Common Core Standards in Language, Speaking and Listening, Foundational Skills, and Writing. They can, as well, support the explicit teaching of metacognitive strategies. The chart on the following page, Focus Points for Follow-Up Standards-Based Lessons (Figure 8.1), is intended as a place to begin. But many other points could also be identified based on the dictates of the text and the needs of your students.

When the Focus Is on the Metacognitive Strategies

Rather than focusing on a standards-based comprehension *skill* in a follow-up lesson (something you want students to be able to demonstrate at the end of their reading related to the Common Core), you may prefer to go back to the text to work on a particular comprehension strategy or on the integration of multiple strategies, addressing the processes by which students build their comprehension. I've worked with comprehension strategies a great deal over the years and believe that there are more effective and less effective ways of helping students think about their thinking as they read.

My book *Constructing Meaning Through Kid-Friendly Comprehension Strategy Instruction* (Boyles, 2004) shows how I make explicit strategy instruction "kid-friendly." You can explore this book to learn an easy-to-implement means of explaining, modeling, and practicing the strategies, guiding students toward independent strategy use. My book *Rethinking Small-Group Instruction in the Intermediate Grades* (Boyles, 2010) also contains a substantial part of a chapter related to reinforcing reading through the use of comprehension strategies. Essentially, I do not think it is effective to teach lesson after lesson on an individual metacognitive strategy. This sends the unintended message to students that the goal is to get better at using the *strategy*. Rather, we need to keep the intent squarely focused on the *meaning* of the text: How can a particular strategy help us to understand a text's meaning more thoroughly?

To that end, I believe our strategy instruction needs to be guided by three basic principles:

- Provide **strategy labels** that are used consistently from classroom to classroom in your school, with language students easily understand. It's helpful when words are already within their meaning vocabulary. For example, most students in Grades 3–6 have a very limited understanding of the definition of "synthesis." But if you ask them to "figure out" something, they know just what you mean. You can always refine the language later for greater precision as students become more proficient strategy users.

- Strategies are most effective when students learn to **integrate** them and apply them in a **discussion** as they talk with peers about text. This, as noted

Figure 8.1

Focus Points for Follow-Up Standards-Based Lessons

College and Career Readiness Standards for Reading (Comprehension)

Standard 2

Theme/main idea, summary, and paraphrasing

- How to identify the lesson/moral/theme in a story and how the author shows this message through the events that take place

- How to identify the main idea in an informational source showing cause and effect between events, actions, or details

- How to paraphrase key parts of a text

Standard 3

Characters/people

- How to identify character/personal traits and how they impacted a story or real-life situation

- How to show how a character/person develops or changes over time

Setting/context/place

- How to explain the impact of time and/or place on a story or event

- How to identify elements of the setting (time and place)

Problem

- How to identify the main problem in a story or real-life situation

- How to identify various kinds of conflict and how these contribute to events or outcomes in a story or real-life situation

  o Character/person vs. self

  o Character/person vs. character/person

  o Character/person vs. nature

  o Character/person vs. society

Standard 4

Words

- How to understand and apply content words to demonstrate understanding of informational texts

- How to determine how word choice contributes to the tone of the text

- How to identify author's craft such as word choice, similes, personification, and metaphors, noting the impact of these on meaning within the text

Standard 5

Text structure/genre/syntax

- How to identify how an author crafts the beginning of a text to capture readers' attention
- How to identify how an author builds suspense throughout a text
- How to identify how an author ends a text in a meaningful, interesting way
- How to identify how an author links parts of a text together
- How to identify the elements of a text that support its structure (e.g., all the story parts in a problem/solution text, the sequence of events in a sequential text, the main idea and details in an expository text)
- How to identify the <u>genre</u> of a text and its genre features
- How to explain how the use of print conventions such as the placing and shaping of print, repeated lines and phrases, and circular text adds to meaning

Standard 6

Point of view/purpose

- How to identify the points of view of two different characters/people within the same text
- How to identify the point of view of a first-person narrator
- How to identify what's important to an author (nonfiction)
- How to explain how the story would be different if it were told by another character

Standard 7

Diverse forms of text (digital, live, film, etc.)

- How to determine the impact of illustrations/graphics on text meaning in literature
- How to determine the role of informational text features in enhancing meaning in informational text
- How to apply viewing skills to the study of digital or media text

Standard 8

Reasoning and rhetoric—just informational text; most substantially applied at Grade 6 and above

- How to determine whether the author's argument presents sufficient evidence that is valid and reliable
- How to apply skills to read like a scientist, historian, or mathematician

Standard 9

Text-to-text connections

- How to compare two characters in a single story
- How to compare two versions of the same story
- How to compare two texts based on a common theme
- How to synthesize information from multiple sources
- How to compare a traditional print version of a text to a nonprint version

(Continued)

(Continued)

Writing

Standard 1: How to write an opinion/argument piece in response to one or more texts

Standard 2: How to write an informative/explanatory piece in response to one or more texts

Standard 3: How to understand and apply Tier 2 (robust) words in speaking and writing

Standard 5: How to rewrite a portion of the text or extend the text by including various author's crafts

Language

Standard 4: How to clarify the meaning of unknown and multiple meaning words and phrases based on the text

Speaking and Listening

Standard 1

- How to engage in an academic discussion based on the text
- How to participate in a collaborative partner or small-group activity based on the text

Foundational Skills

Standard 4: How to read a portion of the text with dialogue or evidence of characters' or people's feelings with accuracy, appropriate rate, and good expression

in Chapter 1, is well aligned to the research-based approach described as "transactional strategy instruction" by Michael Pressley (Pressley et al., 1992).

- When you do teach a specific strategy, remember that what you are really teaching is ***how.*** For example, the end result may be that a student forms a detailed picture in her mind. But the real work of strategic thinking is identifying *how* we know when it's appropriate to make a mental image while reading, *how* to visualize using all our senses, and so forth.

While my work with comprehension strategies preceded the Common Core by several years, the principles noted above are well suited to close reading. To help you apply these principles in close reading follow-up lessons, I provide three resources.

To identify and define metacognitive strategies in an accessible manner, please make use of Figure 8.2, Kid-Friendly Comprehension Strategy Guide. The left column of this chart lists the metacognitive strategies that I find most critical for intermediate-grade readers, labeled in terms students can easily understand. The right column gives key criteria for the strategy with the most important words highlighted in bold font.

I also provide Figure 8.3, Thinking About Thinking in Complex Text: Using Comprehension Strategies Together in Close Reading. This is a discussion guide

Figure 8.2

Kid-Friendly Comprehension Strategy Guide

The Strategies	What They Mean
Noticing	• Close readers are good **observers**. What details do you notice in the text that seem important to its **meaning**? • What details that you notice relate to **what** the author has written (the content)? • What details that you notice relate to **how** the author has written (crafted) the text?
Picturing	• What pictures can you make in your mind based on **details** in the text? • Where are you **inspired** to create a picture in your mind? Why?
Wondering	• What did you wonder about as you read this text? What leads you to think this is **something important** to wonder about? • Are there **serious issues or problems** raised in this text: What do you think the *author* wanted you to wonder about as you read this?
Predicting	• If it's a story, can you predict what might **happen next** based on what you already know about a character, the problem, or some other aspect of the story? • If it's informational text, can you predict the **consequences** of an event or situation? • Are there places in the text where the author builds **suspense**, encouraging you to predict?
Figuring out	• Can you put all the important parts of the text together to **summarize** it? • What does the author **show**, but not *tell* directly? What **clues** lead you to this **conclusion**?
Connecting	• What is the author's **message** or the **main idea** of this text? • How can this message make a difference to what you think or do **from this point forward in your life**?

Available for download at **www.corwin.com/closerreading**

Figure 8.3

Thinking About Thinking in Complex Text

Using Comprehension Strategies Together in Close Reading

1. What details seem especially important to **notice** in this part of the text? Are they surprising in any way? Why might the author have included them? (Be sure to also consider details about the crafting of the text such as the placing and shaping of print, word choice, repeated lines and phrases, etc.)

2. Where in this part of the text do you think the author wants you to **visualize** something? What makes this a good place to visualize (or form mental images)? What senses contribute to your understanding here?

3. Are there any places in this text (or this part of the text) where the author presents problems or issues to **wonder** about? What are the problems or issues? Why might these be important to the meaning of the text?

4. Where in this part of the text do you think the author wants you to make a **prediction**? Why is this a good place for a prediction? (Your prediction might have to do with what happens next, or cause and effect)

5. Is there any place in this part of the text where clues to meaning come together and help you **figure out** something important? What are the clues that led you to this understanding? What have you figured out?

6. Think about the author's central message or the main idea of this text. What does it mean to you in your own life? Can you make a **connection** to how this message or main idea may guide what you do or think in the future?

Available for download at **www.corwin.com/closerreading**

especially well suited to small-group work to help students use comprehension strategies *together*, in an integrated fashion, to process text. Notice that in keeping with the Common Core's focus on the text itself, these strategy focus points ask students to consider the way the author has crafted the text as they seek places within their reading to apply strategies.

Finally, so you can more easily select teaching points for instruction around individual metacognitive strategies when that is in order, I give you Figure 8.4, Focus Points for Comprehension Strategy Lessons. Note that within this chart I specify *how* to approach the text using the strategy (e.g., *noticing*), *what* to notice in both literary and informational text, and for other strategies, *where* to look for a good picture to visualize, question to wonder about, or connection to make.

About Those Personal Connections

Students' personal connections have gotten a bad rap over the last few years because of the inconsequential connections they often make. We know that making personal connections to text does not appear anywhere in the Common Core Standards themselves. However, we also know that connecting meaningfully to a text can help a book resonate with a reader. So what shall we do?

I like to think of the "connections" students make before reading more as "coincidences." If you've been white water rafting and bring your experiences to a text on this topic, so much the better. But in my view, the very best connections occur *after* reading as students ponder the theme, message, or essential question raised by the text: Will your experience with this text change you in some way in the future—how you think about something or act in a particular situation? This is when reading becomes truly transformative: the ultimate connection.

Scaffolding Explicit Instruction

Regardless of how we arrive at our skill or strategy follow-up, we need to pursue it with all the know-how that goes into the development of any skill or strategy— beginning with an explanation of its *purpose*, followed by modeling, and then guided practice that gradually releases students to independence.

There are two types of follow-up we should *always* incorporate:

- Making connections between and among texts
- Providing opportunities for writing

I will discuss each in greater detail below.

Making Connections Between and Among Texts

We now have to see double (or triple) as we plan literacy experiences for our students. One text will never be enough to meet Common Core expectations since performance tasks without exception ask students to combine knowledge from at least two—and probably three or four—texts to respond to a range of questions.

Figure 8.4

Focus Points for Comprehension Strategy Lessons

Each bulleted point can be the focus of a small-group lesson aimed at enhancing students' use of individual metacognitive comprehension strategies. In each case, strategic thinking is supported by helping readers recognize *how* to apply the strategy and *where* the strategy will most likely be applied in the text. You might be able to include more than one point in a lesson.

NOTICING

How to Be a Good "Noticer"	What to Notice in a Story	What to Notice in Informational Text
• Pause as you read • Have an "inner conversation" about what you are reading (or think aloud if that works better for you). • Underline parts of the text that seem important to you. • Use sticky notes to remind you about something you think is important. • Write notes in the margin • Be selective—don't underline *everything*. • Jot thoughts and reactions in a reading journal. • Go back and reread to enhance general understanding. • Use one or more comprehension strategies to keep your mind engaged. • Stay focused on your reading; if you get distracted, you'll miss lots of important clues.	• Characters' names • What a character cares about • Special features about the setting where the story takes place • Something odd that you didn't expect to happen • The turning point • Great words that you might want to use in your own writing • The way the author gets you hooked on the story • The way the author builds suspense • What the author did to make the ending memorable • The way the illustrations make the story even more powerful • The way the author organized the story (is it problem/solution or first, next, then . . . ?) • When something doesn't make sense • Places where the author is hoping you'll picture or wonder or use another thinking strategy	• Names of people—especially if something is written about them • Dates—especially if something is written about them • Bulleted lists • Words in italics or bold font or bigger font • The number of paragraphs about one topic (more paragraphs probably means this is important) • Graphics (they let you know what is important on that page) • Captions—you can get a lot of good information without reading a whole lot • The first paragraph of every article, the last paragraph of every article, and the first sentence of each paragraph • The questions at the end of the chapter—these let you know important points you should look for as you read • Words that you don't understand

PICTURING

How to Make Good Pictures in Your Mind	Where to Find a Good Mental Picture
• Pretend you're making a movie or drawing a picture: What would you put in this scene? • Try to picture—the expression on someone's face, a person's body language, the tone of voice. • Identify a snapshot in the text. • Describe the image in your own words (paraphrase). • Use all of your senses to "see" the picture. • Extend the picture: What else could be in the picture that the author doesn't mention? • Recognize the specific words that help you see the picture in your mind.	• Passages with lots of describing words or action words • Passages where someone is talking or people are having a conversation • Passages where people are expressing some kind of emotion—like yelling at each other, crying, or showing happiness or excitement • Passages that make you laugh—or cry • Passages that remind you of something that happened to you • Passages that are about something scary • Passages that are so important that they stick in your brain even when you don't want them there

WONDERING

How to Ask a Good Question About a Book	Where to Find a Good Question
• Remember the question words (*who, what, when, where, why, how*). • Think: Is this a question that will really help me to understand this [story] better? • Is this a question that needs more than a one-word answer (like *yes* or *no*)? • Consider: What kinds of things does the author want me to wonder about? • Good readers often wonder why characters behave in certain ways; this leads to better understanding of the story. • If you think of a question that you could answer on your own without reading the [story], it probably isn't a good question to be asking about the text. • Questions that make you infer are usually more important than questions with answers that are right in the book.	• Books about something unfair or something that is troubling in some way will probably lead to lots of really important questions. • Informational books about topics you know *something* about, but not *a lot* about will lead to questions about other things you'd like to know. • The title of the book, the picture on the cover, or the blurb on the back may lead to some good questions *before* you read. • Wondering about what will happen next often leads to good questions (and predictions) *during* reading. • Sometimes a story ends before it feels "finished." This is a good place to wonder what would probably happen next. • At the end of a book about a topic that is very troubling, good readers often wonder what makes people/characters behave so badly.

(Continued)

(Continued)

PREDICTING (GUESSING)

How to Get Good at Predicting	Where to Make a Prediction When You Read a Story	Where to Make a Prediction When You Read Informational Text
• Most important: when you read a *story*, you predict what will *happen*. When you read a *nonfiction text*, you predict what you will *learn*. • Make sure your prediction makes sense: Did something that already happened lead to your prediction about what will probably happen next? (Your prediction shouldn't just be what you *want* to happen.) • Sometimes the title helps you predict what will happen in a story, but sometimes the title is more confusing than helpful. Don't spend too much time making predictions based on a title. • It is always good to notice who the author is because if you know the author, you can usually make some good predictions about what the book will be like. • If you know what kind of text you're reading, you'll be able to predict something about it. For example, if you know the story is a *fable*, you will try to predict the *lesson*. • Think about where the author wants you to predict. For example, is there a "cliff-hanger" at the end of a chapter? Does the author build suspense before the mystery gets solved?	• Before you read the story when you check the title, the author's name, and the blurb on the back • Before you read when you think about what the genre is • During reading when you think about what will probably happen next • After reading when you think about what could happen if the author added another paragraph or chapter	• Look at the title. That will give you a *general* idea of what you will learn. • Look at the table of contents (especially the titles of the chapters). That will give you *specific* ideas about what you will learn. • Look at the bolded subheadings in a chapter and try to turn each subheading into a question. That will help you predict what you will learn about in that part of the text. • Look at the graphics (maps, photographs, diagrams, etc.). These will also let you predict what you will learn about.

FIGURING OUT

How to Figure Out	Where and When to Synthesize (Summarize and Combine Information)	Where and When to Infer
• In both stories and informational text, there are things the author wants you to understand even though he or she doesn't tell you	• As you're reading a story—keep summarizing it in your mind to make sure you are understanding the story so far.	• While you read—infer when you want to make a prediction about what might happen next.

How to Figure Out	Where and When to Synthesize (Summarize and Combine Information)	Where and When to Infer
directly; you have to look for clues as you read and figure out the meaning on your own.	• When you've finished the story—summarize to make sure that you know all the story parts (characters, setting, problem, etc.) or that you know the events in sequence when it is not a problem/solution text.	• While you read—infer when you want to figure out how a problem will get solved.
• There are different ways to "figure out" the meaning of a text		• While you read—infer when you are trying to understand a character better.
• You can add up all the clues and figure out how all the pieces fit together. That is one way to *synthesize.*	• When you are reading nonfiction—summarize to figure out the main idea (summarize the details and see what they all have in common).	• While you read—infer as you try to figure out why the author included a particular line or paragraph.
• Another way to *synthesize* is to figure out how information from more than one text fits together: What is the same?	• When you have read more than one text about a topic and want to combine all the information you've learned into one "file in your brain"—summarize with information from both sources.	• While you read—infer whether the author is trying to convince you of something.
• Or you can figure out the "big idea"—the message the author wants you to get as you read the words. That is *inferring.*		• While you read—infer what the text is starting to be about (you can infer about the big idea and theme after reading, too).
		• After reading—infer when you want to figure out the author's purpose for writing the text.

CONNECTING AND REACTING

How to Make Good Connections or Share Thoughtful Reactions	What Kinds of Connections to Look For	What Kinds of Reactions to Look For
• Don't try to connect right at the beginning of the text.	• Experience: What is the "big" experience that the author wants you to think about? Has something like this ever happened to you?	• What was your first impression of this book?
• Figure out the "big idea" as you read before making a connection.		• Did your impression change as you continued to read?
• Make a connection to the "big idea."	• Feeling: What is the feeling that the author wants you to understand? When have you felt this way?	• Overall, how do you rate this book? Why?
• Do not make a connection just to your background knowledge; that is a *coincidence.*	• Theme: What lesson can people in general learn from the experience described in this book? When has this lesson been important in *your* life?	• What was the best part of this book?
• Choose your own detail that matches the big idea—not the same detail the author chose.		• What surprised you?
		• What disappointed you?
• Your reaction will come from your *heart* more than your *mind*; think about your *feelings.*	• Would you like to know the character?	• What could the author have done to improve this book?
	• Would you like to have a similar experience?	• What made you keep reading?
	• Who else would like this book? Why?	
	• Is there another book that reminds you of this book in some way? How?	

When your focus is text-to-text connections, begin with an *anchor* text. This text should provide the foundation and framework for the topic. Even if students did not have access to a companion text, this one should give them quite a thorough understanding of the topic at hand. Then choose texts that elaborate or build on one or more characteristics of the anchor text. For example, if your topic is the phases of the moon, you might want to begin with *Faces of the Moon* (Bob Crelin), which explains lunar phases in language that intermediate-grade students can understand. To add dimension to students' comprehension, you could follow up with the *Moon Gazers' Wheel* (also devised by Bob Crelin), which helps children apply their new moon knowledge step-by-step using a handheld wheel as they gaze into the night sky. For a literary connection, you could try Robert Louis Stevenson's "The Moon" (pictures by Tracey Pearson). Alternatively, some companion texts might offer additional information about one aspect of the anchor text. For texts that express an opinion, you might even locate a second text with a contradictory or conflicting perspective so students can compare and contrast points of view.

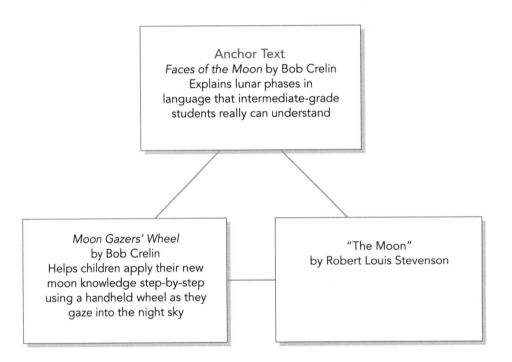

Once you've selected your texts, you will want to read and digest each one separately with your students before making connections between them. Choosing short pieces with a clear connection point will move this process along efficiently. In the case of our *moon* text set, students would first need to realize that although there are many things we could learn about the moon (its topography, moon explorers, and so forth), *Faces of the Moon* focuses on different phases of the moon: new moon, first quarter moon, full moon, and last quarter moon. Of course, you want students to be able to explain some of the facts about each phase, too.

After exploring *Faces of the Moon*, rather than handing them the next text—in this instance, the intriguing little *Moon Gazers' Wheel*—and telling them how these two texts connect, it can be even more powerful to distribute the wheel, explore it a bit together, and then ask, "So what's the connection here?" They should be able to tell you that this "text" will help them *do something with* (apply) the knowledge from their first text. Making these connections themselves is a significant part of students' learning.

For an entirely different spin (but not a different focus), move to Pearson's picture book of Robert Louis Stevenson's poem "The Moon." It begins, "The moon has a face like the clock in the hall," and continues its imaginings as if *this* full moon was shining down upon a quaint seaside village. Maine? (That works for me.) The contrast will work for students, too, as they see that their anchor text *Faces of the Moon*, while also told in rhyme, creates a wholly different feeling from that evoked by Stevenson's classic poem:

> The squalling cat and the squeaking mouse,
> The howling dog by the door of the house,
> The bat that lies in bed at noon,
> All love to be out by the light of the moon.

> —From "The Moon" by Robert Louis Stevenson
> in *A Child's Garden of Verses*, 1885

Think outside the box as you select resources to support your anchor text, and get creative with the kinds of connections you propose—but make sure the connection to the anchor text is a significant one and that students grapple with the connection in a meaningful way. We want to prepare them well for Common Core assessments that may specify tasks such as these:

> Based on the excerpts provided from *Maniac McGee* and *Pippi Longstocking*, show how authors use characters' names to show something important about them as people.

> Choose an American symbol and show how it represents Benjamin Franklin based on the two articles provided about symbols and the story of Franklin's life. Be sure to cite your sources as you supply evidence.

Provide Opportunities for Writing to Sources

Teachers with a close watch over the Common Core will also make sure that their literacy instruction ties a writing task to their anchor text. "Writing to sources" will be a major component of performance tasks—opinion/argument pieces, essays that explain or inform, or full-length narratives. For every text or text set you teach, try to envision at least one writing task, preferably two, that extends students' thinking about the work they've read. You may not *use* both tasks, but you will want to weigh the pros and cons of each before deciding which one is the better fit. In particular, try to identify lots of opinion/argument pieces the students might write. Not only is this a text type that hasn't been explored extensively at the elementary level, but it also promotes the kind of critical thinking that the Common Core encourages for college and career readiness. To facilitate your contemplation of the reading-writing connection, a template for Writing to Sources is provided in Figure 8.5.

Reasons for Revisiting Our Text

There are several reasons for returning to "She Was *THAT* Kind of Lady" for deeper study. While students would likely acquire quite a complete picture of Gram in their first reading, coming back to this narrative to look more closely at the words that contribute to the tone of the text would lead to important insights into the narrator and how she feels about Gram. What students won't really see in their first close reading is that this text is as much about the narrator as it is about Gram. With a closer look, you discover the author's point of view: why she holds her grandmother in such high regard. Does this make Gram an "everyday hero?" Students can have their own opinions about that once they have absorbed the text's full meaning.

Opportunity for Writing. There is a good opportunity here for an opinion piece: In your opinion, was Gram an "everyday hero?"

Connection Between Texts. As I said above, we should *always* find a companion text and a point of connection for students to consider. For me, the picture book *Ma Dear's Aprons* by Patricia McKissack immediately came to mind. The personality traits of the main character bear a striking resemblance to Gram in our narrative, though in this story, you can find a variety of "everyday heroes." Of course, many texts could serve this same purpose.

A sample weekly plan based on the anchor text, "She Was *THAT* Kind of Lady" is provided in Figure 8.6, along with a blank weekly planning template in Figure 8.7. You can use the blank to plan *your* week of instruction using a close reading anchor text. Note that the suggested follow-up skill lessons in Figure 8.6 are for "She Was *THAT* Kind of Lady" and are not intended to prescribe the skill lessons that *you* will need or the order in which you should teach them as you plan a week of your own instruction.

Extending Close Reading Into Small-Group Instruction and Independent Reading

Close reading instruction, as it has been explained to this point, has been mainly described in relation to whole-class shared lessons, where the teacher teaches the lesson to the entire group. But close reading should also be part of our small-group instruction and independent reading. Let's examine close reading first within small-group instruction.

Figure 8.5

Writing to Sources

Title of text(s): _____

This text is useful for

___ a **narrative** piece (writing a **story** or **personal narrative** in relation to a specific incident within the text or a story that **extends** the text or a portion of the story written from another character's perspective)

___ an **informative/explanatory** piece (writing a piece that **explains** important points about a topic, including **insights** and **implications** of the information)

___ an **argument/opinion** piece (writing that takes a critical stance and **defends** a point of view while also **refuting** conflicting points of view)

Task for _____ **writing**

Task for _____ **writing**

Figure 8.6

Planning for a Week of Shared Instruction Based on a Close Reading Anchor Text

(Sample)

Day 1	Day 2	Day 3	Day 4	Day 5
Focus: Close reading of the anchor text	**Focus:** After-reading follow-up	**Focus:** Revisit text: Reading Standard 6 (point of view)	**Focus:** Reading Standard 9 (text-to-text)	**Focus:** Connect to Writing Standard 1 (argument)
Objective: Read for deep understanding: "She was THAT kind of Lady" If necessary, complete the reading on Day 2 before moving to the after-reading tasks.	**Objective:** Complete the reading from Day 1 (if necessary); complete the after-reading tasks, including talking it out for text structure and genre.	**Objective:** Reread the text to determine the author's point of view: How does the author feel about Gram? Why? What is the evidence?	**Objective:** Read an excerpt from Ma Dear's Aprons by Patricia McKissack. In what ways is Ma Dear similar to Gram? In what ways is she different? What is the most important trait they have in common?	**Objective:** In your opinion, was Gram an everyday hero? Defend your opinion with evidence from the text. (Or write a similar opinion piece about Ma Dear)

Figure 8.7

Planning for a Week of Shared Instruction Based on a Close Reading Anchor Text Template

Day 1	Day 2	Day 3	Day 4	Day 5
Focus:	Focus:	Focus:	Focus:	Focus:
Objective:	Objective:	Objective:	Objective:	Objective:

Available for download at **www.corwin.com/closereading**

Small-Group Instruction

Small-group instruction is a good place for students to become "doers." With only five to seven children sitting around a table, there is plenty of opportunity for interaction, even with fairly short group sessions of approximately twenty minutes. It would be ideal if all students could engage in this small-group work around close reading a couple of times per week (though, hopefully, they will have more small-group meetings overall).

Close reading is close reading. The scaffolding suggested for before, during, and after reading during whole-class shared instruction is exactly what we need for close guided reading in small groups, too. But now we need to pay attention to instructional level. Two points need clarification here: *guided reading* and *instructional level*.

Guided Reading. I hesitate to use the term *guided reading* because it conjures up a vision of a particular model of instruction that in general is not well aligned to the intermediate grades and in particular is not a good match for close reading. That said, the goal of small-group instruction is to *guide* the reading of students more closely than can reasonably be accomplished in whole-class instruction where the student-teacher ratio is much higher. For the intermediate grades, I sometimes use the term *guided reading* synonymously with *small-group instruction* because in the best sense, we are *guiding reading* in our *small group*. We are guiding students in the application of the same skills and strategies we introduced in our whole-class shared lessons, but now the text is something they can read more capably themselves.

For close *shared* (whole-class) reading we are using many texts that we know full well are beyond the capacity of some students to handle on their own. This can work because we are offering lots of support. Truth to tell, shared reading is aimed most squarely at teaching students how to *think* about a text. Now, in small-group instruction, they need to apply this thinking to texts more in line with what they can actually *read*. This is where instructional level will be important.

Instructional Level. The Common Core, with its emphasis on complex texts, is asking us to rethink what we mean by "instructional level." Could we provide students with small-group experiences that expect more of them as readers than our data sometimes suggest? I think we can—and should. *If* students can read the text reasonably fluently with few or no decoding problems on each page and *if* the content is appropriate—not too conceptually advanced for their age—then the poem or short story or informational piece is probably worth a try. You may want to use carefully selected longer texts as well. You won't read the whole text (chapter book or informational text) in the close manner described earlier in this book; it would take *months*. But you could extract particular parts rich in meaning or craft and read those portions closely as you come to them. You could even return to these passages later to note all of the meaning you may have missed the first time around.

The first chapter of a literary work is often a good candidate for close reading as it will help students explore the setup of the story. Powerful passages in the middle of the book may demonstrate the building of suspense, and selections from the end will show how an author ties everything together. Similarly, a methodical analysis of the introduction of an informational text is always good for close reading, as it establishes the organizational plan and becomes a great frame of reference as students progress through the content under various subheadings or in different chapters: How does the information under the first heading or in the second chapter (or any specific part) connect to the big picture?

Recently I had the opportunity to do some close reading with a small group of fourth graders. They had just completed the chapter book *On My Honor* by Marion Dane Bauer. The emotional momentum of this story propels it forward as events play out (tragically), taking most students by surprise. Together we went back to the very first page of this text and reread it closely, this time noticing all of the clues the author provided there hinting at the ultimate outcome. Students were amazed that they had missed so many of these details initially. "This is kind of like a scavenger hunt," one student offered. "Nice analogy," I responded. "There's usually a lot to 'scavenge' at the very beginning of a text. I wonder what clues will lie hidden among the words on the first page of your *next* book?"

While there may now be less difference between the texts read by various groups in your class, there should be *some* difference. The Common Core makes scant mention of differentiation, a troubling aspect of these standards for many teachers—and with good reason. We know that just *wishing* that all students could read complex text at grade level will not make it so. The practice of placing difficult text in front of all students during whole-class shared reading will not make it happen either—if that's all we do. Small-group instruction is one of the ways we can pursue this accelerated progress that the Common Core asks of our students, as we ramp up the challenge bit by bit. Our other means of getting there will be through students' independent reading.

Close Independent Reading

While we need whole-class and small-group instruction for introducing and reinforcing principles of close reading, none of this will make much difference unless we also make time for large quantities of independent reading. This is not "SSR" (Sustained Silent Reading) or "DEAR" (Drop Everything and Read) as in days of yore, where students grabbed any book that struck their fancy and read it (or not) for the duration of time allocated to this activity.

The "new" independent reading is more integrated into the fabric of our literacy curriculum. We want students to read to build stamina and enjoyment of reading. But we also want their reading to be purposeful. I don't envision students painstakingly reading their entire independent reading book word by word,

The Common Core makes scant mention of differentiation, a troubling aspect of these standards for many teachers.

phrase by phrase to extract every nuance of the author's meaning. What I see goes something like this:

> Today during independent reading, I want you to find one paragraph (or other small text segment) that you think is important to your text, and ask yourself our four "good reader" questions. When we return to reflect on our reading, I will ask you to share your thinking about the answers to these questions for your text chunk.

This allows the focus to remain on reading for enjoyment but reminds students that good readers also tune in to the important parts of a text in order to understand them deeply. Students will have their close reading bookmark to guide them (see Chapter 7) and perhaps a reading log for tracking their progress—without a lot of writing required. As one example of the way this can look, see My Reading Log in Figure 8.8, with space for a quick notation about attention to close reading. As we look toward our ultimate goal of college and career readiness, this final stop along the journey to independence is, oh, so important. Too often, our gradual release of responsibility stops just short of this final destination.

Monitoring independent reading can (and should) occur as we confer with students. We need to rethink this, too, in light of close reading. Part of the "research" we do as we initiate the conference should be to reflect with the student on the four now-familiar good reader questions: *What is the author saying? What are the hard or important words? What does the author want me to understand? How is the author playing with language to add to meaning?* We should also help students set goals for the reading they do each month, guiding them gently toward a wider range of genres and texts that may be more intellectually challenging than those they've selected in the past. Donalyn Miller is my go-to person for inspiration and ideas for independent reading. I love her books: *The Book Whisperer: Awakening the Inner Reader in Every Child* (Miller, 2009) and *Reading in the Wild*: *The Book Whisperer's Keys to Cultivating Lifelong Reading Habits* (Miller, 2013a). She is also a regular contributor to the blog *Nerdy Book Club* (http://nerdybookclub.wordpress.com), which is a wonderful source for finding out about new books to recommend to your students. In fact, Donalyn is part of the reason I'm always broke; I can't let someone else have a great book that I don't have too. The conferring protocol in Figure 8.9 will get you started as you think about helping your students navigate their independent reading in a meaningful way.

Figure 8.8

My Reading Log

Month of: _____

Name: _____   **Date:** _____

My reading goal for this month is: _____
_____

My Close Reading Questions

1. What is the author telling me here?

2. What are the hard or important words?

3. What does the author want me to understand?

4. How does the author play with language to add to meaning?

Date	Book/Text	Close Reading Passage	I have thought about my *close reading passage* and can answer all four questions (yes or no).

 Available for download at **www.corwin.com/closerreading**

Figure 8.9

Conferring Protocol for Close Reading

1. **Research**: Ask why this chunk was chosen. Ask the four "good reader" questions. What does the student do well? Not so well?

2. **Compliment**: Be specific about something you notice the student doing: "I really like how you put the information on this page into your own words. Good readers do that."

3. **Decide**: Select a teaching point related to the student's needs based on the "good reader questions" or another close reading strategy that is relevant to the text—something the student is right on the verge of understanding.

4. **Name the teaching point with a SKILL and a STRATEGY:** "If you want to decide the most important words [skill], here's how I'd go about it: [strategy].

5. **Demonstrate:** Model how you'd apply the strategy yourself by thinking aloud so the student can see how you would use a particular strategy or question.

6. **Give the student a chance to try it**: Let the student practice applying the strategy as you look on. You will need to (quickly) find a passage where the strategy can be applied.

7. **Inquire:** Ask the student how he or she will apply this strategic thinking in *other* books. (Remember: teaching is about transfer!)

 Available for download at **www.corwin.com/closerreading**

When DIGGING DEEPER IN CLOSE READING Goes Off Track

I see three potential problems as we attempt to dig deeper in close reading:

1. Imbalance. We all tend to overemphasize the instructional format that works best for us. A potential danger of whole-class close reading is that once we get the hang of it, we may be happy to keep the lesson going beyond the allotted thirty minutes, even though it is taking time from small-group instruction and independent reading. This will undermine the reinforcement and application of close reading strategies. On the flip side, too much time on small-group instruction or independent reading without systematic shared close reading instruction will fail to build the competencies students need to apply close reading more independently.

2. Lack of coherence. Another cause for concern as we deepen and connect close reading is that it may not lead to the kind of coherence that the Common Core tells us is so important. If we neglect to reread text to dig deeper, if we fail to connect texts to each other or to writing or to integrate close reading with other Common Core English Language Arts Standards—we will be missing the mark in showing students how everything about their lives as readers and writers can come together in a logical and aesthetically consistent manner.

3. Neglecting narrative writing. Earlier in this chapter, I made the point that we need to make sure we're extending close reading by incorporating opinion and argument writing, which may be new to students. But as we do that, we cannot overlook our old favorite, narrative writing. Just because many intermediate-grade students have had a few years of exposure to this text type does not mean that they do this kind of writing well. And *writing well* is the operative term here. Remember that within narrative writing, craft is especially important. Unless we spend time really *teaching* craft and then providing opportunities for students to *apply* this knowledge to their own writing of stories (and other text types, too), students will not meet Common Core's rigorous Writing Standards 4, 5, and 6. These are the standards that address "how" we write.

From a Week of Study to a Unit of Study

What we can integrate and synthesize over a week, we can extend even further into units of study with text sets that revolve around the close reading of several complex texts. In Chapter 2, I noted that our close reading text, "She Was *THAT* Kind of Lady," might be the first text in such a sequence, and I specified what those other texts might be. Elaborating on that is the work of unit development, which is beyond the scope of this book—though certainly a worthy long-term goal. If students can attain a greater depth of knowledge with a single anchor text and one or two relevant companion texts, just imagine the complex thinking generated by several related anchor texts studied over a month or more! (My next book will provide teachers with actual close reading lessons organized around text sets.)

Before moving to the final chapter of this book for some closing thoughts on close reading, take a few minutes to contemplate the following questions.

Reflecting on What We Know

1. Will scheduling be an issue for you as you find a place for close reading in your literacy curriculum? If so, how can you move other curriculum components around to make room for this? Discuss and share ideas.

2. Is your classroom's physical environment arranged to accommodate close reading for whole-class shared lessons, small-group instruction, and independent reading? How can you maximize the use of space to better meet your students' close reading needs? Discuss and share ideas.

3. Do you think that close reading has a place in students' independent reading? Why or why not? If you do think it has a place, how do you see it fitting in? Discuss your ideas.

4. Examine the chart on page 132 (Figure 8.1), Focus Points for Follow-Up Close Reading Lessons. Consider what areas of need the children in your class typically demonstrate. What skills and strategies might you want to focus on next?

5. Using the same text you used in previous chapters, now plan your close reading follow-up lessons using the blank template in Figure 8.7, Planning for a Week of Shared Instruction Based on a Close Reading Anchor Text.

6. What was hard about doing the above? What was easy? What questions do you have about designing this part of your lesson? Share and discuss your work here with your group—or with at least one other colleague who is also working on close reading.

CHAPTER 9

Close Reading for the Common Core—and More

Instructional Shift

With the Common Core	With the Common Core—and MORE
Value: We have high standards, complex texts, and close reading to guide students toward college and career readiness.	**Value added:** We also need priorities *beyond* the Common Core: positive habits of mind and social consciousness.

The Instructional Shift

We need not look to the past but to the future to understand this shift. The Common Core has given us standards, encouraging teachers and students to aim high. The Common Core has given us complex text, celebrating rich literature and diverse sources of information. The Common Core has given us close reading, inspiring rigorous teaching and deep learning. We acknowledge that these will all contribute to students' college and career readiness. They will be necessary.

But will they be sufficient?

What the Common Core has *not* given us for the English Language Arts is a sense of the context in which standards, complex texts, and close reading will thrive. Before heading down this final Common Core pathway, see Figure 9.1, Ten Steps to Implementing Close Reading, for a quick step-by-step review of close reading instruction as outlined in the previous chapters.

Reflecting on a Close Reading Lesson

We can turn these ten steps into an assessment tool for considering the quality of our close reading lessons. Figure 9.2, Reflecting on a Close Reading Lesson, provides specific criteria to help us reflect on our instruction *before, during,* and *after* a close reading lesson. This guide may be used by teachers for their own self-assessment or by administrators or coaches as they work together with teachers to build capacity in the teaching of close reading. You can also find this chart at the book's companion website (**www.corwin.com/closerreading**).

Adding Value to the Common Core

Students will not meet these standards in a vacuum. Good teachers realize that it's their literacy priorities *beyond* the Common Core that create an environment in which standards flourish.

They recognize that the best close readers will be those who demonstrate not just the *skill* but the *will* to approach texts thoroughly and thoughtfully. The finest teachers of all take steps to prepare their students not simply for college and career but to become responsible citizens of the world. Reaching toward these goals will not shortchange the Common Core; it will add value.

Remember Our Literacy Priorities

We need to remind ourselves that there is life beyond the Common Core. The best close reading in the world and unwavering commitment to standards won't really matter unless this work is embedded in a literacy curriculum that embraces a full range of literacy experiences to which our children can have access on a regular basis. Richard Allington and Rachael Gabriel (2012) cite six experiences they believe every student should have every day:

- Every child reads something he or she chooses.
- Every child reads accurately.
- Every child reads something he or she understands.
- Every child writes about something personally meaningful.
- Every child talks with peers about reading and writing.
- Every child listens to a fluent adult read aloud.

Good teachers realize that it's their literacy priorities beyond the Common Core that create an environment in which standards flourish.

The finest teachers of all take steps to prepare their students not simply for college and career but to become responsible citizens of the world.

Figure 9.1

Ten Steps to Implementing Close Reading

1. **Identify a text you *think* will be suitably complex and engaging for close reading**

   - Could be a picture book, poem, nonfiction article, short story (fable fairy tale, myth, legend, etc.)

   - Consider: Do students have sufficient background knowledge to read the text meaningfully?

   - If not, identify now another text to *build* background knowledge.

2. **Analyze the text for complexity.**

   - If you can, find the Lexile.

   - If not, get another readability measure.

   - Consider qualitative measures of complexity.

   - There should be *some* "very complex" qualitative features—but *all* features should not be complex for any one text.

3. **Determine what you want students to learn from a first close reading.**

   - Be realistic—but a bit aggressive.

   - First reading will probably focus on story parts, factual information, and observations about content and words.

   - You might not get to examine a lot of writer's craft or deep inferences on a first close reading.

4. **Decide how you will approach your text—and chunk it.**

   - How big should the chunks be? Why?

   - Will it be useful to read the entire text first, or will you go chunk by chunk? Why?

   - How will you help students prepare themselves for close reading?

5. **Create text-dependent questions for each chunk—but aim for INDEPENDENCE.**

   - Remember that those text-dependent questions will be your backup plan.

   - Teach students to ask the four "good reader" questions themselves.

   - Be prepared with specific questions in case you need them.

   - Think about the standards in relation to each question—and be sure you're working toward all relevant standards.

6. **Embed your close reading lesson within a week of shared reading instruction.**

   - About 30 minutes per lesson in the intermediate grades

   - What related lessons will follow for depth and breadth?

   - What kind of writing task and text connection can be included?

(Continued)

7. **Identify your (shared) lesson content for the rest of the week**

   - Identify your objective.

   - Also think about lesson length, materials, and procedures.

8. **Consider implications for small-group instruction.**

   - "Close reading" is one priority for small-group instruction, but some lessons should also reinforce skills that students need.

   - Use instructional-level materials—but more complex than past practice.

   - Focus on acceleration—not just remediation.

9. **Consider implications for independent reading.**

   - Must be a consistent part of the literacy block (for stamina, application, enjoyment).

   - Hold students accountable to "close reading" criteria.

   - Try to balance literary and informational text—and many genres.

10. **Embed a week of close reading into a unit of 20–30 days.**

    - This is actually the easy part!

    - Consider developing units and text sets that are both theme and standards based.

    - (Get good at close reading lessons first.)

 Available for download at **www.corwin.com/closereading**

As we've learned from previous chapters, our close reading instruction will speak to many of these points; we just can't forget that experiences from this list that may *not* specifically address close reading are still important. In fact, it's not even *these* particular experiences that are the issue here. Your list of nonnegotiables may contain a few additional items. For example, my list would include the opportunity for students to interact with diverse learners around literacy—working side by side with students of different abilities, students from other cultures, or those just learning English and students with different learning styles and strengths. I would also like technology use incorporated in some way, both as a tool in the learning process and as a mode of self-expression in the products students create.

Figure 9.2

Reflecting on a Close Reading Lesson

Teacher: _____ Coach/Administrator: _____

Text: _____ (This text is/is not suitably complex for these students)

Before Reading

Sets purpose: Identifies lesson *purpose* as deep comprehension of the text rather than designating an isolated objective	
Identifies clues to meaning: Helps students prepare for close reading by considering clues on book cover or in page layout	
Clarifies meaning to seek within the text: Helps students identify text components to look for during reading	
Quick pace; limits input: Completes prereading quickly, without activating/building unnecessary prior knowledge, personal connections, or predictions	

During Reading

Models: Models thinking where needed to demonstrate identification of text elements	
Pauses after short chunks: Pauses <u>frequently</u> during reading to ensure close monitoring; text chunks are <u>short</u>	
Prompts: Prompts students to ask their own good reader questions; gradually releases responsibility to help students become <u>independent</u> close readers	
Text-dependent questions: Asks appropriate text-dependent questions that address <u>many</u> standards; incorporates a line of questions leading to higher-level thinking; not all Standard 1 (evidence)	
Words: Helps students word-solve as needed (both decoding and vocabulary)	

(Continued)

(Continued)

After Reading (*may occur during a follow-up session)

Useful words: Helps students identify useful words for talking about the text*	
Theme/main idea: Helps students infer author's message*	
Gist statement/summary: Helps students create brief gist statement/summary*	
Structure/genre: Helps students identify text structure and genre*	
Oral collaboration: Provides opportunity for oral collaboration for text-dependent task*	

Lesson length:

_____ Seemed appropriate for these learners

_____ Too short (more like a minilesson)

_____ Too long for these students

_____ Too long for the overall length of the literacy block (took too much time away from small-group instruction, independent reading, etc.)

Strengths of the lesson:

Areas for continued growth:

Support requested by the teacher:

Other:

 Available for download at **www.corwin.com/closerreading**

Remember That Close Reading Will Be a Matter of Skill and *Will*

One significant factor that the Common Core neglects in its conversation about college and career readiness is that it's not just the *ability* to read closely that is aligned with success but also students' *willingness* to engage in this kind of serious reading. Costa and Kallick (n.d.) propose sixteen habits of mind that are essential for student success, regardless of the path they choose.

Of course, every one of these habits is important, but I'd like us to think especially about the five that I think have a particularly strong connection to close reading:

1. Successful students *persist*. They focus on the task and complete it successfully. They know how to proceed when they get stuck. Persistence is critical to close reading. If students are going to be successful with complex text—or in any endeavor in school and beyond—they need to stick with it, even when the going gets rough. They need a "can-do" attitude and the resourcefulness to problem-solve when an early attempt at understanding falls short.

2. Successful students *strive for accuracy and precision*. They know what level of precision is appropriate to the task and the subject area, and they are able to increase their precision and accuracy accordingly. Close reading requires much precision. It is not about getting the reading done quickly with a few general impressions. It's about laser-sharp analysis and spot-on conclusions that accurately reflect the author's meaning.

3. Successful students *think and communicate with clarity and precision*, both orally and in writing. They are specific in their communications, and they avoid generalizing, dismissing, and distorting ideas. This is the kind of communication—clear, honest, and precise—that we hope will grow out of close reading. This is what we want students to practice during the oral, collaborative group work preceding written response.

4. Successful students *manage impulsivity*. They control themselves and act thoughtfully and deliberately in any situation. With the need for sustained concentration that close reading requires, we can imagine the struggle that students will face if focus is a problem.

5. Successful students *create, imagine, and innovate*. They look for different ideas and are able to generate original ideas of their own. We hope that our close reading instruction leads to outcomes such as these. We hope that students don't read simply to gain knowledge but to do something positive with the information and understanding that come from their reading. We hope they become responsible citizens of the twenty-first century.

Remember That We Need Strong Citizens of the Twenty-First Century

One deficit of the Common Core in my view is that it proposes college and career readiness as its ultimate aim without any mention of what we want students to be ready to *do* with the complex texts they have read and the close reading they have done over time. I would like to think that beyond preparing students for more book learning, we are also preparing them for the world they will inherit.

Will they be prepared and inclined to *do* something with the knowledge they have gained? I hope that our close readers of today will look back on their education, even their elementary school years, and conclude that those complex texts they labored to read have somehow made a positive difference, not just to their own well-being but to the well-being of others.

So in addition to the rigor that close reading inspires, I hope that through the Common Core we will promote three other *r*'s—relevance, respect, and responsibility. I hope the texts we choose for close reading will help us examine our past and present for themes such as these:

I hope that through the Common Core we will also promote three other r's—relevance, respect, and responsibility.

- Confronting and combating prejudice and inequity
- Creating sense of community
- Taking action for causes that matter
- Developing a positive identity in the twenty-first century
- The importance of remembering and hoping

Moreover, I hope that we as educators will have the fortitude to guide students toward these goals, not just by making the necessary changes to our instructional practices but also by the dispositions we bring to this work. There are plenty of naysayers out there—folks who say it can't be done, individuals who claim that close reading is sure to devolve into dry, boring lessons that will put kids to sleep and turn them away from books forever. I feel sorry for these glass-half-empty people because apparently they have never had the kind of teacher who has helped them recognize that academic rigor can be engaging. Perhaps even exciting. And dare I say it: JOYFUL!

Yes, joyful. In the introduction to this book, I promised you a *joyful* journey into close reading. I hope that the intervening pages have brought you a few steps closer to that goal.

Now, instead of a list of questions to reflect further on what we know, I end this book with just one question for you to explore with your colleagues:

What would it take to teach close reading so well that we would meet the challenges of the Common Core while also achieving other goals that lie at the heart of literacy teaching and learning—as well as goals that reside deep within the hearts of our students?

Appendix I
Templates for Designing Close Reading Lessons

Preparing for Close Reading

Title of text: _____

Curriculum Connection

Reasons for selecting this text:

Theme connection/inquiry question:

Placement of this text within a lesson sequence:

Complexity of the Text

Lexile (if available) or other readability measure:

Qualitative complexities of this text:

Challenges for students reading this text:

Learning Points From the First Close Reading

Approaching the Text

_____ Teacher reads entire text aloud first, then goes back and reads chunk by chunk

_____ Students read entire text first for a general impression; then the teacher reads chunk by chunk

_____ Teacher reads by chunk without an initial read-through by either the teacher or the students

_____ I have determined appropriate text chunks: places to pause and ask questions.

Available for download at **www.corwin.com/closereading**

Planning for Close Reading

Text: _____

Purpose: Deep understanding of the text

Before Reading

Clues based on cover illustration—or . . . :

Clues based on page layout (columns, stanzas, bolded words, etc.):

Clues based on title, author:

Probable text type (literary or informational), possible genre:

During Reading

Questions students should ask themselves for each chunk of text:

- What is the author telling me?
- Any hard or important words?
- What does the author want me to understand?
- How does the author play with language to add to meaning?

Follow-up: Text-dependent questions for the teacher to ask about each chunk of text:

First chunk:

Second chunk:

Third chunk:

(Continued)

(Continued)

<table>
<tr><td>Fourth chunk:</td></tr>
<tr><td>[Add additional chunks as needed]</td></tr>
</table>

After Reading

(Depending on time available, some tasks below may not be completed on same day as first close reading)

<table>
<tr><td>

Follow-up tasks for close reading:

1. Important words to talk about the text:

2. Theme/lesson/message:

3. Summary or gist statement:

4. Structure and genre:

5. Optional: Additional task related to this text or students' skill needs:

Talk it out:

[Written task]

</td></tr>
</table>

Appendix II
Sample Lesson Plan for Shared Reading: "She Was *THAT* Kind of Lady"

Text Selection and Preparation for Close Reading

Title of text: She Was *THAT* Kind of Lady

Curriculum Connection

Reasons for selecting this text: Good example of a personal narrative; shows depth of character as a text of this sort should; shows the impact of the setting on the person; reasonably complex for fourth graders.

Theme connection/inquiry question: What qualities do you admire most in a role model or everyday hero?

Placement of this text within a lesson sequence: This text would work well as an initial lesson because it addresses a topic to which students can relate while exploring a new theme/inquiry.

Complexity of the Text

Lexile (if available) or other readability measure: 1070; Flesch Kincaid: 5.2

Qualitative complexities of this text:

- Knowledge demands: No connection to small town New England life in the early part of the twentieth century
- Meaning: Gram is a complex character to understand—her own values and her impact on others
- Language: Lots of unfamiliar vocabulary: succotash, (Cadillac) fins, house dresses, wringer washing machine
- Structure: Text is nonlinear; not a problem/solution structure

Challenges for students reading this text:

N/A without knowledge of the particular class

Learning Points From the First Close Reading

- A mental image of the setting—time and place
- Understanding of Gram as a person and what was important to her
- The way Gram interacted with other people
- The meaning of "She Was *THAT* Kind of Lady," and its connection to a theme about Gram as a generous, kind, simple woman

---

Approaching the Text

____ Teacher reads entire text aloud first, then goes back and reads chunk by chunk

____ Students read entire text first for a general impression; then the teacher reads chunk by chunk

_X_ Teacher reads by chunk without an initial read-through by either the teacher or the students

_X_ **I have determined appropriate text chunks: places to pause and ask questions.**

Lesson Planner for Close Reading

Text: "She Was *THAT* Kind of Lady"

Purpose: Deep understanding of the text

Before Reading

Clues based on cover illustration—or . . . :

N/A

Clues based on page layout (columns, stanzas, bolded words, etc.):

- The text is broken into parts that are numbered (shows how much to read at one time; where to pause to think)

Clues based on title, author:

- *Was* lets you know this is in the past; It sounds like this lady is no longer living
- Notice the word *lady*—so this must be about a woman, a grown-up
- Notice the word *THAT* is written in all capital letters and it's in italics, so it must be important too.
- When you say someone is *that* kind of boy or *that* kind of girl, you usually have some trait or behavior in mind that you're referring to; Look for *that* "behavior or trait for this lady

Probable text type (literary or informational), possible genre:

- No clues to indicate this is informational, so it's probably literary; can't tell the genre

---

During Reading

*Reading anchor standards are identified in parentheses next to each question

---

Questions students should ask themselves for each chunk of text:

- What is the author telling me?
- Any hard or important words?
- What does the author want me to understand?
- How does the author play with language to add to meaning?

Follow-up: Text-dependent questions for the teacher to ask about each chunk of text:

First chunk:

- Who is telling this story? (granddaughter) (1)*
- What do you know about this lady so far? (many details provided) (1)
- What does the author want you to understand? (Grandma wasn't "cool," but this doesn't seem to be a bad thing.) (3)
- What strategy do you think the author wants us to use here? Why? (picturing; lots of details to create picture in your mind) (5)

(Continued)

(Continued)

Second chunk:

- What word does the author repeat in the first couple of sentences that stands out? Why do you think the author repeats these words? (plain; plain is a good word to describe Gram) (5)

- What are the details in this section mostly about? (1) (doing the wash)

- Doing the wash isn't very exciting. Why do you think the author spent so much time describing this? (shows that Gram's life wasn't very exciting by most standards; helps us in understanding the time period) (3)

- Does the author seem to be telling the story here from the point of view of a child or an adult? What makes you think this? (child's point of view; long-ago memories) (1)

- What about the last line of this chunk? Are you beginning to understand what *"that"* means? (The author used a line from this chunk as the title; seeing that Gram is a simple and good lady) (5, 2)

- What are you learning in this chunk about Gram's point of view on life? What makes you think this? (didn't need fancy things; liked her old ways) (6)

Third chunk:

- What are you learning about Gram here? (worked in the family grocery store 43 years; gave granddaughter popsicle) (1)

- What is the author trying to show us here? (Gram's generosity) (3)

- How many people in Gram's life have you met so far? (2—Pop and granddaughter) (1)

- What does it mean to give someone "a hand"? (help them out) (4)

Fourth chunk:

- What is this chunk mostly about? (the food Gram made) (1)

- Why is the word *real* in quotes? (Some people don't consider staying home and cooking a "real" job.) (5)

- What senses does the author want us to use here? (picturing, smelling) (5)
  What words lead us to these senses? (peaches, roast beef, fried chicken, pickles) (4)

- Any words you don't understand here? (maybe *Victorian, succotash, pie face, chili sauce, lemon meringue*) (4)

- Are you beginning to get a more complete picture of this time and place? Describe it. (3)

- How does this chunk fit with the Chunk 3 above? (both about Gram's hard work and generosity) (5)

- Do you have anything to add for *that* kind of lady? (generosity, thoughtfulness) (3)

Fifth chunk:

- What is this section mostly about? (driving) (1)

- Does this change your thinking about Gram? How? (Gram liked to feel special, important; although she mostly fulfilled traditional female roles, she was strong, smart independent.) (3)

- What words lead you to this new thinking? ("felt like a queen"; Cadillac; perched; guided; didn't mind being alone) (4)

Sixth chunk:

- What is the author giving you information about in this chunk? (1) (Gram and her porch)
- The author uses hyperbole (exaggeration) in this chunk and also in the chunk above. What is getting exaggerated? Why is the author doing this? (longest fins in the world; every problem in the universe—makes the point that the fins were *really* big and there were *lots* of problems (4)
- Does this part confirm anything you already know about "*that* lady"? Does it add anything new? (confirms *generosity*; adds *friendliness*) (3)

Seventh chunk:

- What details is the author sharing here? (rice pudding, smile) (1)
- What does it mean to "collect people"? (lots of friends) (4)
- Why do you think the author included this information? (She was kind to others, so they were kind to her (6)

Eighth chunk:

- What is happening in this part of the text? (Gram is telling stories to her great granddaughter) (1)
- What interesting punctuation do you see at the beginning of this chunk? What are these called? What is the author trying to show here? (ellipses; showing the passing of time) (5)
- How can you tell time has passed? (little girl now was the great granddaughter) (1)
- Why does the author include these stories (more details about Grams' simple life; hardships; small details that were memorable to her; showed Gram's point of view—that she just accepted that life was like this, even the disappointing parts; she didn't complain) (6)

Ninth chunk:

- What are you finding out here? (granddaughter and family now lived with Gram) (1)
- Why does Gram call herself "the old gray mare"? What is she referring to when she says this? (This refers to the old song lyrics: "The old gray mare, she ain't what she used to be..." Just like the old gray mare, Gram feels old.) (9)
- Again the author repeats the line, "She was *that* kind of lady." What kind of lady is that? (many traits evident by now) (3)

In this part of the text you get a more direct view of the granddaughter's (author's) feelings about her grandmother. What are those feelings and how are these feelings shown? (feels lots of love; moved in to care for her and her house) (2)

After Reading

(Depending on time available, some tasks below may not be completed on same day as first close reading)

Follow-up tasks for close reading:

1. **Important words to talk about the text:**

    (whole class—quick oral response)

    Words *in* the text: Gram, porch, old fashioned, people, stories

    Words *about* the text: generosity, kindness, admired

(Continued)

2. **Theme/lesson/message:**

(turn and talk with partner; whole class share)

Theme about Gram:

- Happiness comes from the simple things in life and from giving to others;

Theme about the granddaughter:

- Sometimes the people we admire most aren't those who accomplish great deeds, but those who live their lives with kindness toward others.

3. **Summary or gist statement:**

(whole class—quick oral response)

Create a gist statement:

- A kind, generous grandmother who was happy with simple things in life was loved and admired by her family and friends.

4. **Structure and genre:**

(small group collaborative activity; see "Talk it out" below)

Memoir: A collage of memories about someone special to the author, showing how the subject related to the time and place in which she lived, and the important people in her life

5. **Optional: Additional task related to this text or students' skill needs:**

Not included for this initial close reading

Talk it out:

Noticing Text Structure and Genre (complete template in small groups)

[Written task]

Not included for this initial close reading

Appendix III
Templates for *After* Reading

Most Important Words

My name or my group: _____

Text: _____

Choose _____ words *in* the text that you feel are the most important.
     (number)

This word is important	because . . .

Choose _____ words ***about*** the text that you feel are the most important.
     (number)

This word is important	because . . .

Available for download at **www.corwin.com/closerreading**

Template 2

Theme Chart

Theme	Book 1	Book 2	Book 3	Book 4	Book 5

Available for download at **www.corwin.com/closerreading**

Gist Statement and Brief Summary

My name or my group: _____

Text: _____

Gist Statement

1. Identify the **who** or **what** in your text.
2. Think about what is **most important** to remember about this text.
3. Make up a sentence with this information of no more than **20 words**.
4. Practice saying it until it sounds **smooth**.

_____

_____

Four-Sentence Summary of a Story

1. What **message** does the author want us to remember about this story?
2. What happens at the **beginning** of the story to show this message?
3. What actions or events in the **middle** of the story show this message?
4. What happens at the **end** to show this message?

_____

_____

_____

_____

Four-Sentence Summary of an Informational Text

1. What is the **main point** the author is making in this text?
2. What is **one detail** that shows this point?
3. What is a **second detail** that shows this point?
4. What is a **third detail** that shows this point?

_____

_____

_____

_____

Noticing Text Structure and Genre

My name or my group: _____

Text:_____

The structure of this text is: _____

(Some possibilities: problem/solution, sequence of events, main idea and details, compare/contrast, cause/effect, descriptive)

Draw a quick diagram of the text structure in the box below:

```
┌─────────────────────────────────────────────────────┐
│                                                       │
│                                                       │
│                                                       │
│                                                       │
│                                                       │
│                                                       │
│                                                       │
│                                                       │
└─────────────────────────────────────────────────────┘
```

The genre of this text is:_____

(Some possibilities: fairy tale, fable, realistic fiction, historical fiction, mystery, myth, legend, science fiction, fantasy, biography, "all about," "how to" literary nonfiction)

Genre characteristics:

One genre characteristic present in this text is: _____

Example: _____

_____

A second genre characteristic present in this text is: _____

Example: _____

_____

A third genre characteristic present in this text is:_____

Example: _____

_____

_____

Evidence From First Close Reading of a Text

My name or my group: _____

Text: _____

Important words to use to talk about this text:

Gist (one main idea sentence) **OR summary** (Theme sentence and 3 detail sentences):

Three genre characteristics of this text and examples:

Other useful observations or insights for informational text: The way one event or step led to another; the way the author used language; point of view; graphics; validity and reliability of this source; text-to-text connections

---

Other useful observations or insights for literary text: Story parts; the way the author used language; point of view; illustrations; text-to-text connections

---

Paraphrase It!

PARAPHRASE IT!

Name: _____ **Date:** _____

Prove that _____

_____

In the text it says: "_____

_____."

I can say this in my own words: _____

_____

PARAPHRASE IT!

Name: _____ **Date:** _____

Prove that _____

_____

In the text it says: "_____

_____."

I can say this in my own words: _____

_____

Words That Show Tone

My name or my group: _____

Author's Craft	Examples From the Text
Strong verbs (action words)	
Interesting adjectives and adverbs (describing words)	
Similes (compare with *like* or *as*)	
Metaphors (something *stands for* something else)	
Personification (describing something that is not human as if it *were* human)	
Idioms (expressions like *it's raining cats and dogs*)	
Sensory images (things you can see, hear, taste, smell, feel)	
Other phrases or words	

Looking Into Illustrations

My name or my group: _____

The illustration I/we are studying: _____

1. What part of the story is this illustration from? How does that make a difference?

2. What feeling do you get from this illustration? What creates this feeling?

3. Why do you think the author/illustrator included this illustration? How does it contribute to the overall message of the text?

4. How does this illustration contribute to the mood or tone of the text?

5. Why do you think the author/illustrator chose these colors or this particular style for this illustration?

6. For informational text: How does this illustration/graphic add to your understanding of this content?

7. If you were illustrating this scene, how would your illustration be different from the one the author/illustrator created? Why would it be different?

8. Is there anything about this illustration that you think misrepresents the subject or promotes stereotypes?

Template 9

Viewing a Video

My name or my group: _____

Title of the video: _____

The Message

1. What is the message?

2. Who is the message for?

3. What is the purpose of the message?

4. What have I learned about the topic?

5. What were the key words or concepts?

6. Whose point of view is presented?

The Medium

1. How did different images capture your attention?

2. What was the most interesting visual element? Why?

3. What individuals are most often represented in the media and what individuals (e.g., gender, culture, age) are absent?

4. Who owns or supports this medium (e.g., television, newspaper, Internet) and why might this matter?

Template 10

Reading a Photograph

My name or my group: _____

Observe

A. Look carefully at the photograph. What was your first reaction? Why?

B. What do you see in this photograph?

People	Objects	Activities

Make an Inference

Based on what you have observed in the photograph, list three things you might infer or conclude from this image.

1.

2.

3.

Next Steps

1. What questions does this image raise in your mind?

2. Where could you find answers to them?

Adapted from Wisconsin Historical Society website: "Using Primary Sources," http://www.wisconsinhistory.org/turningpoints/
primarysources.asp#sensative

Available for download at **www.corwin.com/closerreading**

Evaluating an Argument

My name or my group: _____

The text: _____

1. Is the author a respected authority on the subject? How do you know?

2. Is the source current? If it's a book, what is the copyright? If it's an article, when was it published?

3. What is the author arguing for? (What is the author claiming?)

4. Does the evidence support the author's claims? What is the evidence?

5. Does the author leave you with any unanswered questions? What questions?

6. Is the author fair to all points of view? Explain.

Available for download at **www.corwin.com/closerreading**

Template 12

Reading and Evaluating a Primary Source

My name or my group: _____

Primary source: _____

Think about these questions as you examine this source:

Understanding the Context

1. Who wrote it? What do you know about this person?

2. When was it written?

3. If it was a speech, where was it delivered?

4. What was the reason for this document?

5. If there was an "event," who was probably in the audience?

Understanding the Document

1. What are the most important words, and what do they mean?

2. What point is the author trying to make?

3. What evidence does the author give to support his or her point?

4. Does the author make any assumptions? What are they?

Adapted from Wisconsin Historical Society website: "Using Primary Sources," http://www.wisconsinhistory.org/turningpoints/primarysources.asp#sensative

Available for download at **www.corwin.com/closerreading**

Template 13

Reading Like a Scientist

My name or my group: _____

Text: _____

1. Who wrote this? Is this someone who has a good <u>reputation</u> for understanding science?

2. When was this written? If it was written a long time ago, is this the kind of topic where the information could be outdated?

3. What does this writer know a lot about? What did the writer need to study?

4. Why do you think the writer wrote this?

5. What words from the text would a scientist need in order to talk about this topic?

6. What scientific problem or question is related to this text?

7. What does this writer seem to think about this problem or question? How can you tell?

8. What scientific problem or question should be explored further to better understand this topic?

9. Why is it important to find the *right* answer to this problem or question?

10. How might the answer to this question or solution to this problem change my life or someone else's life?

Template 14

Reading Like a Historian

My name or my group: _____

Text: _____

1. Who wrote this? Do you know anything about this person? Is he or she an expert?

2. When was this written? If it was written a long time ago, is this the kind of topic where the information could be outdated?

3. Which points seem to be the most important here? Why?

4. What evidence does the author use to support these points?

5. Does the author try to *inform* or *persuade* you? If the author is persuading, what "side" does he or she take?

6. If the author seems to be trying to persuade, what words or phrases does he or she use to convince you that he or she is right?

7. What pieces of evidence are the most believable? Why?

8. What pieces of evidence are the least believable? Why?

9. Is there anything that the author said where you think you need more "proof"? Explain.

10. What would it be like to see this event through the eyes of someone who lived in this place during this time?

Appendix IV
Websites for Short Texts

- Project Gutenberg

  www.gutenberg.org

  For any text with an expired copyright; both long and short texts (consider using an excerpt of a longer text)

- EyeWitness to History

  www.eyewitnesstohistory.com

  Firsthand accounts illustrated with vintage photos, original radio broadcasts, etc.

- Famous Speeches and Speech Topics

  www.famous-speeches-and-speech-topics.info

  Short speeches, famous speeches, women's speeches, etc.

- Garden of Praise

  www.gardenofpraise.com

  Short biographies; great for Grades 3–5

- Time for Kids

  www.timeforkids.com

  Current news articles at 4 levels (k–1, 2, 3–4, 5–6)

- EDSITEMENT: The best of humanities on the Web

  www.edsitement.neh.gov

  Lesson plans for literature, social studies, history, art, and culture

- Video clips appropriate for school

  www.youtube.com/schools

  This promises to be a safe site

- ReadWorks

  www.readworks.org/books/passages

  Over 1,000 nonfiction reading passages with associated text-dependent question sets, leveled using the Lexile framework; new passages are added frequently

- Short passages: fiction/nonfiction by grade level; one-page passages

  www.teacher.depaul.edu

  Excellent site with lots of easy-to-find resources

- Classic poetry for children

  www.storyit.com/Classics/JustPoems/index.htm

  There are many possibilities for accessing classic poetry. Here is one to try.

- Twelve poems every student should know (including notes on interpretation)

  http://www.mensaforkids.org/school_template.cfm?showPage=school_poetically.cfm

  These are generally quite difficult poems—but important ones

- Online library of picture books read aloud; words are highlighted as they are read

  http://www.storylineonline.net/

  This is an AOL site for kids.

  Good for primary or struggling intermediate grade readers

- Online library of picture books read aloud

  www.tumblebooks.com

  Click on TUMBLECLOUD junior for books for upper-elementary grade students. Click on TumbleBook Library for younger students.

  Good for primary or struggling intermediate grade readers

- A variety of text types: stories, articles, etc.

  www.storyarts.org/library

  Good site for fables and folktales

- Stories for young children

  www.magickeys.com/books

  Some of these stories include audio

Appendix V
Bibliography of Picture Books for Close Reading

Teachers have asked me repeatedly for a bibliography aligned to the College and Career Readiness Standards for Reading. Here it is! Of course there are thousands of texts that would support any standard. These are the books that happen to be on *my* bookshelf. Please know that they are just examples of the kinds of books that could work to help students reach a particular standard. Do not feel compelled to run out and buy these exact books. Look for books in your school or classroom library that have some of the same characteristics.

The books suggested in the bibliography below are mostly literary texts, though some feature "real people" in stories with a factual base. Whole informational books are generally too complex for a close reading lesson at the intermediate level. For informational text, it is best to use shorter pieces such as articles or passages from a longer text.

Included here are texts you can use to help students practice the skills they will need to meet Standards 2, 3, 4, 5, and 6. Remember that *every* text will help with skills needed to meet Standards 1 and 10 and that the skills needed to meet Standards 7 through 9 will mostly be addressed in follow-up lessons. The standards below are those that are most closely associated with an initial close reading lesson.

Standard 2: Summary, Theme, Main Idea

There are too many great books with great themes to ever list them all. Below are some of the books I use most often. For a more comprehensive list of specific themes and alignment of texts to those themes, see my book *That's a Great Answer* (2nd ed.).

Lower Intermediate

- *Down the Road* by Alice Schertle
- *Each Kindness* by Jacqueline Woodson

- *Frederick* by Leo Lionni
- *A Frog Thing* by Eric Drachman
- *Galimoto* by Karen Lynn Williams
- *Hey, Little Ant* by Phillip and Hanna Hoose
- *Keep Climbing, Girls* by Beah Richards
- *Melissa Parkington's Beautiful, Beautiful Hair* by Pat Brisson
- *Miss Rumphius* by Barbara Cooney
- *Nobody Owns the Sky: The Story of "Brave Bessie" Coleman* by Reeve Lindbergh
- *The Sandwich Swap* by Queen Rania Al Abdullah of Jordan
- *Stand Tall, Molly Lou Mellon* by Patty Lovell
- *Tacky the Penguin* by Helen Lester
- *Those Shoes* by Maribeth Boelts

Upper Intermediate

- *As Good as Anybody* by Richard Michelson
- *A Bad Case of Stripes* by David Shannon
- *Be Good to Eddie Lee* by Virginia Fleming
- *Dave the Potter* by Laban Carrick Hill
- *Dear Willie Rudd* by Libba Moore Gray
- *Dream* by Susan V. Bosak
- *Eggbert, the Slightly Cracked Egg* by Tom Ross
- *The Empty Pot* by Demi
- *Four Feet, Two Sandals* by Karen Lynn Williams and Khadra Mohammed
- *14 Cows for America* by Carmen Agra Deedy
- *The Honest-to-Goodness Truth* by Patricia C. McKissack
- *Jam & Jelly by Holly and Nellie* by Gloria Whelan
- *Just a Dream* by Chris Van Allsburg
- *The Lotus Seed* by Sherry Garland
- *Lou Gehrig: The Luckiest Man* by David A. Adler
- *The Memory String* by Eve Bunting
- *Mercedes and the Chocolate Pilot* by Margot Theis Raven
- *Minty: A Story of Young Harriet Tubman* by Alan Schroeder
- *More Than Anything Else* by Marie Bradby
- *My Rows and Piles of Coins* by Tololwa Mollel

- *Odd Boy Out: Young Albert Einstein* by Don Brown

- *One Thousand Tracings* by Lita Judge

- *The Princess and the Pizza* by Mary Jane Auch

- *A River Ran Wild* by Lynne Cherry

- *The Royal Bee* by Frances Park and Ginger Park

- *Silver Packages* by Cynthia Rylant

- *Something Beautiful* by Sharon Dennis Wyeth

- *Testing the Ice* by Sharon Robinson

- *Thank You, Mr. Falker* by Patricia Polacco

- *Virgie Goes to School With Us Boys* by Elizabeth Fitzgerald Howard

- *Weslandia* by Paul Fleischman

- *The Yellow Star* by Carmen Agra Deedy

Standard 3:
Connecting Story Parts, Details, Facts

The following texts *feature* the attribute indicated (character change, character development, etc.) Remember, however, that what the Common Core encourages most is the *interaction* between story elements. Examine this attribute in relation to other aspects of the text such as setting and problem.

Character Change

- *A Bad Case of Stripes* by David Shannon

- *Fireflies* by Julie Brinckloe

- *Going Home* by Eve Bunting

- *The Honest-to-Goodness Truth* by Patricia C. McKissack

- *The Memory String* by Eve Bunting

- *My Rotten Redheaded Older Brother* by Patricia Polacco

- *A Picnic in October* by Eve Bunting

- *The Sandwich Swap* by Queen Rania Al Abdullah of Jordan

Character Development

- *Be Good to Eddie Lee* by Virginia Fleming

- *Dave the Potter* by Laban Carrick Hill

- *Down the Road* by Alice Schertle

- *Jam & Jelly by Holly and Nellie* by Gloria Whelan

- *Lou Gehrig: The Luckiest Man* by David Adler (significance of problem)

- *Melissa Parkington's Beautiful, Beautiful Hair* by Pat Brisson
- *One Green Apple* by Eve Bunting
- *Salt in His Shoes: Michael Jordan in Pursuit of a Dream* by Deloris Jordan and Rosalyn Jordan
- *The Summer My Father Was Ten* by Pat Brisson
- *Testing the Ice* by Sharon Robinson
- *Tomás and the Library Lady* by Pat Mora
- *Too Many Tamales* by Gary Soto
- *Uncle Jed's Barbershop* by Margaree King Mitchell
- *Weslandia* by Paul Fleischman

Significance of the Setting (a few examples)

Set in a Specific Location

- *All the Places to Love* by Patricia MacLachlan (home)
- *Appalachia* by Cynthia Rylant (Appalachia)
- *Four Feet, Two Sandals* by Karen Williams (Mideast refugee camp)
- *Goal* by Mina Javaherbin (South Africa)
- *Going Home* by Eve Bunting (Mexico)
- *The Lotus Seed* by Sherry Garland (Vietnam)
- *Mama Panya's Pancakes: A Village Tale From Kenya* by Mary Chamberlin and Rich Chamberlin (Kenya)
- *Planting the Trees of Kenya* by Wangari Maathai (Kenya)
- *A River Ran Wild* by Lynne Cherry (pollution of the environment)

Set in the Civil Rights Era or Pre-Civil Rights Era

- *Freedom School, Yes!* by Amy Littlesugar
- *Freedom Summer* by Deborah Wiles
- *Goin' Someplace Special* by Patricia C. McKissack
- *Momma, Where Are You From?* by Marie Bradby
- *The Story of Ruby Bridges* by Robert Coles
- *This Is the Dream* by Diane Z. Shore and Jessica Alexander
- *Uncle Jed's Barbershop* by Margaree King Mitchell
- *White Socks Only* by Evelyn Coleman

Set in World War II or Post-World War II Era

- *Baseball Saved Us* by Ken Mochizuki (Japanese Internment camps)
- *The Bracelet* by Yoshiko Uchida (Japanese Internment camps)

- *Heroes* by Ken Mochizuki (Japanese Internment camps)
- *Luba, the Angel of Bergen-Belsen* by Luba Tryszynska-Frederick (Nazi concentration camps)
- *Mercedes and the Chocolate Pilot* by Margot Theis Raven (Germany, Berlin air lift)
- *One Thousand Tracings* by Lita Judge (aiding German people)
- *Rose Blanche* by Roberto Innocenti (Nazi Germany)

Turning Point

- *The Orange Shoes* by Trinka Hakes Noble
- *The Other Side* by Jacqueline Woodson
- *Sister Ann's Hands* by Marybeth Lorbiecki
- *Those Shoes* by Maribeth Boelts

Surprise Ending

- *Charlie Anderson* by Barbara Abercrombie
- *For the Love of Autumn* by Patricia Polacco
- *Goin' Someplace Special* by Patricia C. McKissack
- *Goldilocks and Just One Bear* by Leigh Hodgkinson
- *Probuditi!* by Chris Van Allsburg
- *The Wednesday Surprise* by Eve Bunting
- *The Wretched Stone* by Chris Van Allsburg
- *The Yellow Star* by Carmen Agra Deedy

Standard 4: Vocabulary, Author's Craft

When you're looking for good word choice, you need to consider what makes the word or words effective. How do the words contribute to the tone or set the mood? Below are several criteria to consider when determining why words in a text are effective.

Writers use words in a variety of ways to create powerful images.

- *All the Colors of the Earth* by Sheila Hamanaka
- *Dogteam* by Gary Paulsen
- *Frederick* by Leo Lionni
- *Hello Ocean* by Pam Munoz Ryan
- *Home Run* by Robert Burleigh
- *Hoops* by Robert Burleigh
- *One Tiny Turtle* by Nicola Davies
- *Scarecrow* by Cynthia Rylant
- *The Seashore Book* by Charlotte Zolotow

- *Snow* by Cynthia Rylant
- *Water Dance* by Thomas Locker

Writers choose names that "fit" for people and places.

- Aunt Tiny, from *Yolonda's Genius* by Carol Fenner
- Fudge (Peter), from *Tales of a Fourth Grade Nothing* by Judy Blume
- Kanga and Roo, from *Winnie-the-Pooh* by A. A. Milne
- Junie B. Jones, from *Junie B. Jones* series by Barbara Park
- The Land of Chew-and-Swallow, from *Cloudy With a Chance of Meatballs* by Judi Barrett
- Maniac McGee, from *Maniac McGee* by Jerry Spinelli
- Miss Bonkers, from *Hooray for Diffendoofer Day* by Dr. Seuss, Jack Prelutsky, and Lane Smith
- Pippi Longstocking, from *Pippi Longstocking* by Astrid Lindgren

Writers choose strong verbs.

- *In the Small, Small Pond* by Denise Fleming
- *A Story for Bear* by Dennis Haseley
- *When Sophie Gets Angry—Really, Really Angry* by Molly Bang

Writers choose striking adjectives.

- *My Mama Had a Dancing Heart* by Libba Moore Gray

Sometimes writers make up their own words.

- *Double Trouble in Walla Walla* by Andrew Clements

Writers create images with similes.

- *My Dog Is as Smelly as Dirty Socks* by Hanoch Piven
- *Quick as a Cricket* by Audrey Wood
- *The Seashore Book* by Charlotte Zolotow

Writers use personification to create images.

- *Dear World* by Takayo Noda
- *In November* by Cynthia Rylant
- *Snow* by Cynthia Rylant

Writers use hyperbole (exaggeration) to create images.

- *Paul Bunyan* (and other tall tales) retold by Mary Pope Osborne in *American Tall Tales*

Writers use words with a "double meaning" to create an interesting effect.

- *Food Fight!* by Carol Diggory Shields
- *Tough Cookie* by David Wisniewski

Writers use figurative language to add to meaning:

- *The King Who Rained, The Sixteen Hand Horse, A Chocolate Moose for Dinner*—or other books by Fred Gwynne

- *There's a Frog in My Throat* by Loreen Leedy and Pat Street

Writers use dialect to give their writing a sense of place.

- *Young Cornrows Callin' Out the Moon* by Ruth Forman

Standard 5: Structure

Text *structure* is perhaps the most complex and misunderstood of all of the College and Career Readiness Standards, for it can imply so many things. We are most accustomed to hearing about this in relation to basic nonfiction text structures: compare/contrast, sequence of events, cause/effect, and so on. But these don't really reflect *craft*—which is the way that the Common Core asks us to think about structure. From the perspective of craft, structure can mean the genre of the text (Why did the author write this as a play, a poem, a letter, etc.?). Structure can also relate to the internal organization and *craft* of a piece of writing: repeated sentences, variation in sentence length, the way the print is placed and shaped on the page, the use of italics, bolded words, and the like. It can also refer to the way an author gets the reader's attention, builds suspense, and ends a story. Several of these crafted elements of structure are noted below.

Format

Play/Dialogue

- *Hey, Little Ant* by Phillip Hoose, Hanna Hoose, and Debbie Tilley

Layers of Meaning (the "main text" and additional details in a smaller font)

- *Bat Loves the Night* (and other books) by Nicola Davies
- *Dream* by Susan V. Bosak

Told in Verse

- *Meet Danitra Brown* by Nikki Grimes
- *Nobody Owns the Sky: The Story of "Brave Bessie" Coleman* by Reeve Lindbergh

Allegory

- *A Bad Case of Stripes* by David Shannon
- *Eggbert, the Slightly Cracked Egg* by Tom Ross
- *The Empty Pot* by Demi
- *Feathers and Fools* by Mem Fox
- *Wings* by Christopher Myers

Letter Text

- *Dear Mr. Blueberry* by Simon James
- *Dear Willie Rudd* by Libba Moore Gray
- *Nettie's Trip South* by Ann Turner

Journal Text

- *Diary of a Worm* by Doreen Cronin
- *Hamzat's Journey: A Refugee Diary* by Anthony Robinson
- *The Wretched Stone* by Chris Van Allsburg

Newspaper Text

- *Extra! Extra!: Fairy-Tale News From Hidden Forest* by Alma Flor Ada
- *Fairytale News* by Colin Hawkins and Jacqui Hawkins

Nonfiction Stories

- *A Caribou Journey* by Debbie S. Miller
- *The Eyes of Grey Wolf* by Jonathan London
- *One Tiny Turtle* by Nicola Davies

Photo Journal

- *In My Family/En Mi Familia* by Carmen Lomas Garza
- *Remember: The Journey to School Integration* by Toni Morrison
- *Snapshots From the Wedding* by Gary Soto

Alphabet Books

- *Allison's Zinnia* by Anita Lobel
- *The Boat Alphabet Book* by Jerry Pallotta—or others
- *The Z Was Zapped* by Chris Van Allsburg

Personal Narrative/Memoir

- *All the Places to Love* by Patricia MacLachlan
- *Appalachia* by Cynthia Rylant
- *Hairs/Pelitos* by Sandra Cisneros
- *Mercedes and the Chocolate Pilot* by Margot Theis Raven
- *Momma, Where Are You From?* by Marie Bradby

Sequence/Life Cycle

- *Giant Pandas* by Gail Gibbons
- *How a House Is Built* by Gail Gibbons
- *Sky Tree* by Thomas Locker

Story-Within-a-Story

- *Aunt Isabel Tells a Good One* by Kate Duke
- *Dinner at Aunt Connie's House* by Faith Ringgold
- *The Seashore Book* by Charlotte Zolotow

Flip Sides

- *Marianthe's Story: Painted Words and Spoken Memories* by Aliki
- *Reflection* by Ann Jonas
- *Round Trip* by Ann Jonas

Pattern Text

- Begin with a question: *Will We Miss Them?* by Alexandra Wright
- Repeating lines and phrases: *When I Was Young in the Mountains* by Cynthia Rylant; *Meanwhile Back at the Ranch* by Trinka Hakes Noble; *I, Matthew Henson: Polar Explorer* by Carol Boston Weatherford; *Tulip Sees America* by Cynthia Rylant
- Circular ending: *My Mama Had a Dancing Heart* by Libba Moore Gray

Structure of Sentences; Use of Punctuation

Writers use a combination of long and short sentences to make their ideas stand out.

- *An Angel for Solomon Singer* by Cynthia Rylant
- *Welcome to the Green House* by Jane Yolen

Writers sometimes begin a sentence with *And*.

- *When I was Young in the Mountains* by Cynthia Rylant
- Many fairy tales ("And they all lived happily ever after.")

Writers sometimes use sentence fragments.

Too many books to note

Alliteration makes writing sound musical.

- *Dinorella* by Pamela Duncan Edwards
- *The Seashore Book* by Charlotte Zolotow

Writers sometimes say something again for emphasis.

- *Dreamplace* by George Ella Lyon
- *The Whales* by Cynthia Rylant

Writers sometimes use *dashes* as another way of showing side comments.

- *Junie B. Jones and Her Big Fat Mouth* by Barbara Park

Writers sometimes use lots of *ands* instead of commas to create a particular effect.

- *The Relatives Came* by Cynthia Rylant
- *Scarecrow* by Cynthia Rylant
- *A Story for Bear* by Dennis Haseley

Writers sometimes use ellipses (dot-dot-dots).

- *Down the Road* by Alice Schertle (shows that the journey goes on and on)
- *The Whales* by Cynthia Rylant (shows that the author doesn't know what to say next)
- Ellipses can also show hesitation or moving from one subject to another

Writers sometimes use colons.

A colon is a signal. Colons can be used in many artful ways to let readers know what is coming in a text. They can show that something big is about to follow. They can show that a list is coming. They can show that someone is going to talk (as in a play script).

Writers sometimes use ALL CAPS to give a word or phrase extra emphasis.

- *Hooray for Diffendoofer Day* by Dr. Seuss, Jack Prelutsky, and Lane Smith
- *Princess Penelope's Parrot* by Helen Lester

Sometimes writers use *italics,* which can show many things.

Italics are used for making noise. Italics are used for emphasizing a particular word. Italics are used to show the thinking that is going on in someone's head. Italics are sometimes used to show someone is talking.

- *Night in the Country* by Cynthia Rylant (and many, many other books)

Writers sometimes present their text almost like a "free verse poem" with interesting line breaks that emphasize words in a particular way.

- *Dave the Potter* by Laban Carrick Hill
- *Dear World* by Takayo Noda
- *The Whales* by Cynthia Rylant
- *What You Know First* by Patricia MacLachlan

Writers sometimes place and shape print in interesting ways to add to the meaning of their text.

- *Come to My Party* by Heidi Roemer (a book of shape poems)
- *I Stink* by Kate and Jim McMullan
- *Madeline* by Ludwig Bemelmans (last page)
- *Tulip Sees America* by Cynthia Rylant
- And so many more . . .

Standard 6: Point of View

Texts that support point of view are those through which you can hear the author's or character's voice. You can tell what is important to the person. You can tell who is talking because the thoughts are unique to that person.

Writers "tell it like it is"—not the way they'd like it to be.

- *Halloween* by Jerry Seinfeld
- *Pictures From Our Vacation* by Lynne Rae Perkins

Narrators who are kids *sound* like kids.

- *Earrings!* by Judith Viorst (or anything by Judith Viorst)
- Junie B. Jones books by Barbara Park (or other books by Barbara Park)
- *Super-Completely and Totally the Messiest* by Judith Viorst

Writers risk talking about "tough stuff."

- *Coming on Home Soon* by Jacqueline Woodson
- *Koala Lou* by Mem Fox

Sometimes there are two or more voices in the same book.

- *Dear Mother, Dear Daughter* by Jane Yolen and Heidi Stemple
- *The Pain and the Great One* by Judy Blume
- *Talkin' About Bessie* by Nikki Grimes
- *Voices in the Park,* by Anthony Browne
- *Town Mouse, Country Mouse* by Jan Brett

Sometimes books are written from a point of view different from what you expect.

- *Cinderella's Rat* by Susan Meddaugh
- *Encounter* by Jane Yolen
- *The Paperbag Princess* by Robert Munsch
- *The Princess and the Pizza* by Mary Jane Auch
- *The True Story of the Three Little Pigs,* by A. Wolf, as told to Jon Scieszka

Sometimes books are written directly to "you."

- *The Secret Knowledge of Grown-Ups* by David Wisniewski
- *The True Story of the Three Little Pigs,* by A. Wolf, as told to Jon Scieszka

Sometimes the narrator is someone *in* the story.

- *Winners Never Quit* by Mia Hamm
- *Momma, Where Are You From?* by Marie Bradby
- *More Than Anything Else* by Marie Bradby

- *Nettie's Trip South* by Ann Turner
- *The Raft* by Jim LaMarche
- *Testing the Ice* by Sharon Robinson
- *The Wretched Stone* by Chris Van Allsburg

Sometimes authors give a voice to things that don't really talk:

- *Atlantic* by G. Brian Karas
- *Dear Mrs. LaRue* by Mark Teague
- *Dogs Rule!* by Daniel Kirk
- *I Stink* by Kate and Jim McMullan
- *Memoirs of a Goldfish* by Devin Scillian
- *Once I Ate a Pie* by Patricia MacLachlan and Emily MacLachlan Charest
- *The Tree That Would Not Die* by Ellen Levine

Writers show their voice through their knowledge of *where* the story takes place or their knowledge of the subject.

- *Alaska's Three Pigs* by Arlene Laverde
- *Antarctica* by Helen Cowcher
- *Earrings!* by Judith Viorst
- *Korean Cinderella* by Shirley Climo
- *The Three Snow Bears* by Jan Brett

Available for download at **www.corwin.com/closerreading**

Works Cited

Abrams, M. H. (1999). New criticism. In *A glossary of literary terms* (7th ed.). Fort Worth, TX: Harcourt Brace College.

Allington, R., & Gabriel, R. (2012). Every child every day. *Educational Leadership, 69*(6), 10–15.

Beers, K., & Probst, R. E. (2013). *Notice & note: Strategies for close reading.* Portsmouth, NH: Heinemann.

BEYOND THE RHETORIC: Improving college readiness through coherent state policy. (n.d.). Retrieved from http://www.highereducation.org/reports/college_readiness/gap.shtml

Blauman, L., & Burke, J. (2014). *The Common Core companion: The standards decoded, Grades 3–5: What they say, what they mean, how to teach them.* Thousand Oaks, CA: Corwin.

Boyles, N. (2001). *Teaching written response to text: Constructing quality answers to open-ended comprehension questions.* Gainesville, FL: Maupin House.

Boyles, N. (2004). *Constructing meaning through kid-friendly comprehension strategy instruction.* Gainesville, FL: Maupin House.

Boyles, N. (2010). *Rethinking small-group instruction in the intermediate grades: Differentiation that makes a difference.* Gainesville, FL: Maupin House.

Boyles, N. (2011). *That's a GREAT answer: Teaching literature response strategies to elementary, ELL, and struggling readers* (2nd ed.). Gainesville, FL: Maupin House.

Burke, J. (2013a). *The Common Core companion: The standards decoded, Grades 6–8: What they say, what they mean, how to teach them.* Thousand Oaks, CA: Corwin.

Burke, J. (2013b). *The Common Core companion: The standards decoded, Grades 9–12: What they say, what they mean, how to teach them.* Thousand Oaks, CA: Corwin.

Coleman, D., & Pimentel, S. (2011). *Publishers' criteria for the Common Core State Standards in English language arts and literacy, grades 3–12.* Retrieved from http://www.edweek.org/media/3-12-criteria-blog.pdf

Coleman, D., & Pimentel, S. (2012). *Revised publishers' criteria for the Common Core State Standards in English language arts and literacy, grades 3–12*. Retrieved from http://www.corestandards.org/assets/Publishers_Criteria_for_3-12.pdf

Costa, A. L., & Kallick, B. (n.d.). *Habits of mind*. Retrieved from http://www.chsvt.org/wdp/Habits_of_Mind.pdf

Fitzgerald, J., & Amendum, S. (2007). What is sound writing instruction for multilingual learners? In S. Graham, C. MacArthur, & J. Fitzgerald (Eds.), *Best practices in writing instruction* (pp. 289–307). New York, NY: Guilford Press.

Frey, N., & Fisher, D. B. (2013). *Rigorous reading: 5 access points for comprehending complex texts*. Thousand Oaks, CA: Corwin.

Harvey, S., & Goudvis, A. (2007). *Strategies that work: Teaching comprehension for understanding and engagement*. Portland, ME: Stenhouse.

Keene, E., & Zimmermann, S. (2007). *Mosaic of thought: The power of comprehension strategy instruction*. Portsmouth, NH: Heinemann.

Miller, D. (2009). *The book whisperer: Awakening the inner reader in every child*. San Francisco, CA: Jossey-Bass.

Miller, D. (2013a). *Reading in the wild: The book whisperer's keys to cultivating lifelong reading habits*. San Francisco, CA: Jossey-Bass.

Miller, D. (2013b). *Reading with meaning: Teaching comprehension in the primary grades*. Portland, ME: Stenhouse.

National Governors Association Center for Best Practices and the Council of Chief State School Officers. (2010a). *Common Core State Standards for English, language arts & literacy in history/social studies, science and technical subjects— Appendix A: Research supporting key elements of the standards*. Washington, DC: Author. Retrieved from http://www.corestandards.org/assets/Appendix_A.pdf

National Governors Association Center for Best Practices and the Council of Chief State School Officers. (2010b). *Common Core State Standards for English, language arts & literacy in history/social studies, science and technical subjects— Appendix B: Text exemplars and sample performance tasks*. Washington, DC: Author. Retrieved from http://www.corestandards.org/assets/Appendix_B.pdf

National Governors Association Center for Best Practices and the Council of Chief State School Officers. (2010c). *English language arts standards, anchor standards, college and career readiness anchor standards for reading*. Washington, DC: Author. Retrieved from http://www.corestandards.org/ELA-Literacy/CCRA/R

Partnership for Assessment of Readiness for College and Careers. (2012). *PARCC model content frameworks: English language arts/literacy grades 3–11*. Retrieved from http://www.parcconline.org/sites/parcc/files/PARCCMCFELALiteracyAugust2012_FINAL.pdf

Paul, R., & Elder, L. (2008). *How to read a paragraph: The art of close reading*. Dillon Beach, CA: Foundation for Critical Thinking Press.

Pearson, P. D., & Gallagher, M. C. (1983). The instruction of reading comprehension. *Contemporary Educational Psychology, 8,* 317–344.

Pressley, M., El-Dinary, P. B., Gaskins, I., Schuder, T., Bergman, J., Almansi, L., & Brown, R. (1992). Beyond direct explanation: Transactional instruction of reading comprehension strategies. *Elementary School Journal, 92,* 511–554.

Robb, L. (2013). *Unlocking complex texts: A systematic framework for building adolescents' comprehension.* New York, NY: Scholastic.

Rosenblatt, L. (1938). *Literature as exploration.* New York: Appleton-Century; (1968). New York: Noble and Noble.

Shanahan, T. (2012, June 18). What is close reading? [Blog post]. Retrieved from http://www.shanahanonliteracy.com/2012/06/what-is-close-reading.html

Taberski, S., & Burke, J. (2014). *The Common Core companion: The standards decoded, Grades K–2: What they say, what they mean, how to teach them.* Thousand Oaks, CA: Corwin.

Text complexity grade bands and Lexile bands. (2013). Retrieved from http://www.lexile.com/using-lexile/lexile-measures-and-the-ccssi/text-complexity-grade-bands-and-lexile-ranges/

Vygotsky, L. (1978). *Mind and society.* Cambridge, MA: Harvard University Press.

Williams, C., Stathis, R., & Gotsch, P. (2008). *Speaking of writing: The significance of oral language in English learners' literacy development.* Ruidoso, NM: Teacher Writing Center.

Index

BECAUSE ALL TEACHERS ARE LEADERS

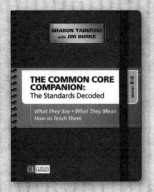

Sharon Taberski

On that grades K–2 *Companion* teachers have been pleading for

Leslie Blauman

On the how-to's of putting the grades 3–5 standards into day-to-day practice

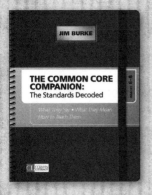

Jim Burke

On what the 6–8 standards really say, really mean, and how to put them into practice

Jim Burke

On that version of the 9–12 standards all high school teachers wish they had

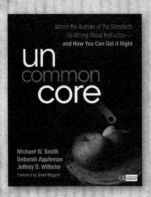

Michael Smith, Deborah Appleman & Jeffrey Wilhelm

On where the authors of the standards go wrong about instruction—and how to get it right

ReLeah Lent & Barry Gilmore

On practical strategies for coaxing our most resistant learners into engagement and achievement

N14E3-B

CORWIN
A SAGE Company